Macroeconomics

Macroeconomics

Second Edition

Volume I

David G. Tuerck

BUSINESS EXPERT PRESS

Macroeconomics, Second Edition, Volume I

Copyright © Business Expert Press, LLC, 2018.

First published in 2015 by
Business Expert Press, LLC
222 East 46th Street, New York, NY 10017
www.businessexpertpress.com

ISBN-13: 978-1-94709-876-3 (paperback)
ISBN-13: 978-1-94709-877-0 (e-book)

Business Expert Press Economics and Public Policy Collection

Collection ISSN: 2163-761X (print)
Collection ISSN: 2163-7628 (electronic)

Cover and interior design by Exeter Premedia Services Private Ltd., Chennai, India

Second edition: 2018

10 9 8 7 6 5 4 3 2 1

Printed in the United States of America.

To the memory of my parents, George and Bertha Tuerck

Abstract

Macroeconomics is the study of the economy as a whole and of the work and saving choices of individual economic agents from which macroeconomic activity emerges. This book, produced in two volumes, takes an integrative approach to that topic. It introduces macroeconomics as a study of (1) the long-run, "micro" foundations of macroeconomic analysis and (2) the short-run deviations from long-run equilibrium that are brought about by disparities between aggregate supply and aggregate demand. The first of these is the subject of Volume I, the second, the subject of Volume II.

The first chapter of Volume I focuses on the importance of a clear understanding of the difference between long-run and short-run analyses of macroeconomic activity, showing, in particular, how confusion over the effects of government deficits on the economy can arise from failing to distinguish between their short-run and long-run effects. Chapter 2 explains the distinction between nominal and real gross domestic product and works through the fundamentals of the National Income and Product Accounts. Chapter 3 lays out a simple model of the work and saving choices of individual economic agents, and Chapter 4 generalizes the analysis to a more sophisticated analysis of the consumption/saving calculus. Chapter 5 derives the supply and demand for labor and for capital, which represent the principal inputs to aggregate production. Chapter 6 takes up the issue of economic growth and reviews some of the current pessimism relating to U.S. economic growth. Finally, Chapters 7 and 8 examine the micro effects on aggregate economic activity of changes in government tax and spending policy.

Volume II begins with a review of monetary policy (Chapter 1) and fiscal policy (Chapter 2) for their impacts on the aggregate economy. Chapter 3 considers at length the distinction between self-correcting and non-self-correcting distortions between aggregate supply and demand. There we review the focus of the Keynesian model on economic downturns brought about by long-lasting excess supply and the focus of the "suppressed inflation model" on long-lasting excess demand. Chapter 4 considers the complexities that arise in diagnosing a decrease in the rate of economic growth that might result from a temporary change in the demand for money or that might be a sign of a more long-lasting secular stagnation. The government's interpretation of this problem will determine whether the growth rate simply adjusts to a new normal or the economy sinks into a protracted downturn. Chapters 5 and 6 examine the Great Contraction of 2007 to 2009 for the lessons that can be learned from it and from recent macroeconomic policy changes.

Keywords

aggregate demand, aggregate supply, classical tradition, monetary and fiscal policy, excess demand, excess supply, full employment, individual equilibrium, Laffer curve, natural unemployment rate, non-accelerating inflation rate of unemployment, non-accelerating inflation rate of labor-force participation, Phillips curve, potential GDP, steady state of economic growth, structural unemployment, supply side economics

Contents

Acknowledgments

I would like to express my appreciation to a few of the many people to whom I am indebted for help in writing this book and getting it into print. First and foremost, as with the first edition, I want to thank my wife, Prema Popat, without whose encouragement and patience the book would never have seen the light of day. Next, my thanks go to Khang Vinh (Kyle) Doan, my undergraduate assistant, and to Xhulia Kanani and William Burke, both of the Beacon Hill Institute, who helped me by finding and verifying data and by proofing much of the book. Also, and as before, Scott Isenberg, Executive Editor at Business Expert Press, provided both patience and encouragement. Exeter team worked efficiently and diligently with me on proof reading and production. Finally, and again as with the first edition, my thanks to colleague Alison Kelly, whose prodding got me to refocus on this project after many years of hesitation and neglect.

CHAPTER 1

Introduction

Macroeconomics is the study of the economy as a whole as distinguished from microeconomics, which is the study of individual consumers, workers, firms, industries, and markets. Microeconomics focuses on the individual economic decision maker (or "agent") without attempting to take into account the full range of interactions that take place between one decision maker and another. Thus, for example, a microeconomic study of an excise tax on the purchase of cigarettes would consider the effect of that tax on the demand for cigarettes but not attempt to account for the effects of that tax on the demand for watermelons and then its feedback effects on the demand for cigarettes.

Macroeconomics is, in essence, a study of feedback effects—of interactions between major economic sectors in response to extraneous events and changes in government policy. It's just that when we do macroeconomics, we don't focus on individual products like cigarettes or watermelons. We focus on major economic indicators such as gross domestic product, the capital stock, and the supply of goods and workers.

At the heart of the question of how these indicators behave is the question of how individual economic agents adjust their actions to changes in government policies and other events that influence their behavior. Even though macroeconomics considers the economy broken down into major sectors, it therefore can take—and here we do take—what is called a "microfoundations" approach to its study. Thus, in studying the labor sector, we first ask how the individual worker adjusts the amount of time he spends working to the reward he gets for working and how the individual saver adjusts his saving to the reward he gets for saving. Only after we understand how the individual adjusts his decision to work and save can we understand how the aggregate supply of labor and the aggregate supply of capital adjust to changes in the rewards for work and saving.

The purpose of any economic system is to provide a mechanism through which buyers and sellers can coordinate their activities to their advantage and in such a way as to exploit as many opportunities as possible for mutual gain. For the most part, and throughout the developed world, it is the marketplace that determines the economic activities of buyers and sellers. There is, to be sure, a great deal of direction that comes from government as well. Every country has a government that engages in its own transactions and imposes taxes to finance those transactions. And in some countries with mostly free economies these transactions account for a large fraction of economic activity. But most of the transactions that take place around the world come about as a result of voluntary exchanges between buyers and sellers. The microfoundations of macroeconomics lie in the decisions taken by individual economic actors to work and save and, at the firm level, to hire labor and engage in capital spending.

This book is divided into two volumes. Both volumes incorporate the familiar economic concept of supply and demand. The difference lies in the separation of the tools of supply and demand for the analysis of two, rather distinct, phenomena: (1) decisions by individuals to supply the services of labor and capital and by firms to employ those services in production and (2) the supply and demand for goods and labor, as impacted by government's monetary and fiscal policy.

Volume I focuses on the first phenomenon: the services of labor and capital as supplied by, and as demanded by, individual economic agents. It provides a framework for understanding the effects of taxes and government spending on individual choices and, through those choices, the aggregate economy. Volume II focuses on the process by which the market system equilibrates the supply and demand for goods and labor and of how government uses monetary and fiscal policy to correct such failures that might occur in that process. It also examines the recent history of U.S. monetary and fiscal policy for their effects on the economy, both during the Great Contraction of 2007 to 2009 and during its aftermath.

The possibility of a major economic downturn such as the Great Contraction has traditionally remained the principal concern of macroeconomists. Indeed, macroeconomics as a field of study came into being from a book called *The General Theory of Employment, Interest, and Money*, written by John Maynard Keynes in 1936, which was motivated by Keynes's interest in how the economic system broke down and deteriorated into a worldwide depression (Keynes 1936).

Keynes did not use the term "macroeconomics"; it was coined later.[1] But he did set the stage for a theory of the economy in which wage and price adjustments that normally keep the economy at "full employment" (a term on which we elaborate in the following) fail and, having failed, leave the economy in a state that calls for government intervention in the form of expansive monetary and fiscal policy. Government policies aimed at correcting for the failure of an economic system to achieve full employment are frequently referred to as "stabilization policies," connoting the idea that it is the job of government to stabilize the economy at a level that brings about full employment without inflation.

Macroeconomics, as presented in most textbooks, is still seen in the spirit of Keynes's book, primarily focused on whether and how government can use monetary and fiscal policy to keep the unemployment rate below some threshold level, say, 5 percent. If the unemployment rate rises above this level, then, according to standard macroeconomic theory, the government should carry out expansive policies that will increase aggregate demand. The goal of stabilization policy, according to most macroeconomists, is to bring about and maintain "full employment," while, at the same time, keeping the rate of inflation low (say, around 2 percent). It's a matter of juggling policy tools to keep aggregate demand at the right level.

The purpose of this book is to show that this view of the macroeconomic problem is dangerously (for the economy) oversimplified. The economic problem, if there is one, can lie on the supply side of the economy, as well as on the demand side. One "supply-side" problem can arise from distortions in the markets for labor and capital that pull down the level of potential, full-employment output. "Supply-side" economics, as traditionally defined, is about removing these distortions with the aim of increasing output. But another supply-side problem can arise as

---

[1] According to macroeconomist Kevin Hoover, the first person to use the term "macroeconomics" was Ragnar Frisch, the Norwegian economist (and future Nobel laureate), in a lecture given in 1931 (Hoover 2008a, p. 332).

well. This problem arises from maladjustments in prices and wages that keep aggregate supply below aggregate demand. Economists refer to this much-neglected phenomenon as "suppressed inflation"—the failure of prices and wages to rise in tandem with a rise in aggregate demand and for firms and workers, as a result, to withhold their products and services from the marketplace.

There are therefore two supply-side problems that can lead to suboptimal performance by the economy: one that arises from distortions in the individual markets for labor and capital and another that arises because of a misalignment between aggregate supply and demand. This requires the economist to compartmentalize his analysis of the macroeconomy. This book attempts to do just that by focusing on distortions (for example, taxes) that negatively affect the flow of labor and capital services into production in Volume I and by focusing on distortions between aggregate supply and demand in Volume II.

One way to simplify matters is to identify a single macroeconomic indicator whose behavior is taken to represent the performance of the overall economy. Here that indicator is "real" (that is, inflation adjusted) gross domestic product (GDP). Real GDP is a measure of the goods and services produced within a geographic unit (here, the United States) in a year's time. This book focuses on the conditions that determine the level of real GDP and on how government measures—or the absence of appropriate government measures—can negatively affect real GDP.

One important concept based on this measure is "potential" or "full-employment" real GDP, which refers to real GDP when aggregate supply is aligned with aggregate demand. We think of this also as GDP when there is full employment, or, more precisely, when the unemployment rate is low enough so that, for all practical purposes, everyone who wants a job has a job.

There are, to be sure, other measures of economic performance. Another, probably superior but less utilized, measure is real GDP per person. Another is real consumption per person. We will consider these alternative measures in due course as we work through the analysis. But we can make our lives easier by thinking of the macroeconomic problem as one of maintaining a high rate of growth of real GDP, given that the quality of economic life is not just about production (and consumption) but also about smelling the roses or, as we will view it, the ability of economic agents to enjoy leisure.

Another simplifying technique is to separate macroeconomics into a short-run and long-run problem. The underlying idea is that, in the long run, the economy gravitates toward full employment, whereas, in the short run it may not. Keynes criticized what he called "classical" economics for not allowing for this difference. As Keynes saw it, an imbalance between aggregate supply and demand might be self-correcting, as classical economics argued, but sometimes it will not (as witnessed in the severity and length of the Great Depression).

When defenders of the classical tradition claimed that imbalances between aggregate supply and demand would be self-correcting, at least in the long run, Keynes famously answered that "in the long run we are all dead." Keynes saw himself as the originator of a new school of economic thought that would force the profession (and politicians) to understand that the "short run" could become very long indeed.

This book sees a distinction between self-correcting and protracted imbalances between aggregate supply and demand. Self-correcting imbalances do not require government intervention through monetary and fiscal policy to bring aggregate supply and demand back into line with each other. Protracted imbalances do.

For some three decades after its publication, Keynes's *General Theory* remained the bedrock of macroeconomics. The working assumption was that policy makers should keep a steady eye on economic indicators like real GDP and the unemployment rate and stand ready to deploy the weapons available to them at any moment to prevent production and employment from falling, while at the same time, keeping an eye on the inflation rate.

Beginning in the late 1960s, however, a counterrevolution was launched that challenged Keynes's ideas. This counterrevolution spawned a "new classical" economics, which argued that Keynes's remedies for a failing economy were likely to be ineffectual and unnecessary. Imbalances would correct themselves, and Keynes's policy tools were likely to be ineffective anyway. This school of thought succeeded in stripping Keynes of much of his intellectual authority, at least until the downturn that began in December 2007. It is safe to say that, until that downturn, the exponents of the new classical economics and their allies from various sub-branches of that line of thinking were carrying the day.

I will state upfront that I subscribe to this new classical school, insofar as I think that it has much to say about improving economic performance, especially through tax and welfare reform. Thus, Volume I of this book is focused on explicating the "new classical" world, in which the economy is performing normally (which is to say, it hasn't broken down owing to imbalances between aggregate supply and aggregate demand) and will respond positively to policy reforms that incentivize people to work and save. Volume II considers policies that are appropriate for correcting protracted periods of low employment and reviews the policies adopted over the span of the recent Great Contraction.

Keynes's core idea was that a sudden, unanticipated fall in the demand for goods could create a state of affairs in which the economy would sink into a long-lasting slump. This fall in demand could come from various sources. The fact that the U.S. money supply shrank by nearly one-third during the Great Depression no doubt helps explain its depth and length. If a downturn occurs because of a fall in aggregate demand, a housing crisis or a related financial crisis, or any other such cause or combination of causes, then the obvious remedy is for government to increase demand through expansive monetary and fiscal policy.

This line of thinking, though presumably invalidated by the new classical economics, sprang phoenix-like from the ashes when the Great Contraction got under way in late 2007. In reality, Keynesian thinking had remained—and remains today—alive and well in the deliberations of the Federal Reserve Open Market Committee, where Federal Reserve officials preside over monetary policy. The architects of the new classical economics—economists such as Robert Barro, Robert Lucas, and Thomas Sargent—had won all the battles but never quite won the war against what they saw as Keynesian dogma.

The new classical economists argued that expansive monetary and fiscal policies will fail in their purpose, since, once those policies are known to have been implemented, individual economic agents will adjust their behavior in such a way as to defeat the purpose for which the policies were implemented. A collateral proposition is that the government should focus its attention not on the demand side but on the supply side of the economy, where, by reducing distortions in economic activity, particularly in the form of taxes, it can improve the performance of the economy. From this point of view sprang the practice of "supply-side economics."

The recognized way of putting the distinction between Keynesian and new classical thinking is to recognize two states in which the economy can find itself. In one state—the classical state—markets clear through appropriate price and wage adjustments, and government can improve economic performance only through the elimination of distortions in individual markets for goods and for labor and capital. (In Volume I, I give a lot of attention to that state.) The other state—the Keynesian state—represents a state in which price and wage rigidities prevent markets from clearing and cause the economy to contract in response to a fall in the demand for goods and labor. The trick is to recognize which state the economy is in and to apply the appropriate remedies. For some economists, it is a matter of distinguishing the short run from the long run.

In an article entitled, "The Economy Needs More Spending Now," economist Alan S. Blinder offered his own characterization of the short-run/long-run distinction (Blinder 2013). "Poor economic policy," he argued, stems, among other things, from "the failure to distinguish between the short-run and the long-run effects of particular policies."

"In the short-run," said Blinder,

> output is demand-determined. The big question is how much of the country's productive capacity is used. And that depends on the strength of demand—the willingness of businesses, consumers, foreign customers and governments to buy what American businesses are able to produce.

The long run, however, is different. "In the long run,...a larger accumulated public debt probably spells higher interest rates, which deter some private investment spending. Economies that invest less grow less" (Blinder 2013).

The problem is that Blinder fails to recognize that interest rates can rise in both a short-run and a long-run scenario involving increased government spending. In the short run, deficits brought about by increased spending can increase interest rates because of the increase in output that they bring about and because of the resulting increase in the demand for money. (We recognize this line of thought in Chapter 3 of Volume II of this book.) In the long run, it is a temporary rise in government spending, which may or may not take place in tandem with a rise in the deficit, that can cause interest rates to rise. (We address this possibility in Chapter 2 of Volume II.)

Blinder's short-run problem arises when the supply of goods and labor exceeds demand: The quantity of labor services demanded by firms is less than the quantity workers want to provide, and the quantity of goods demanded by consumers is less than the quantity firms want to provide.

What Blinder ignores is an equally plausible short-run problem that arises when demand exceeds supply. The economy can suffer a downturn in production and employment because workers offer fewer labor services than firms want to hire and because firms offer fewer goods than consumers want to buy. Chapter 3 of Volume II will show how both scenarios—generalized excess supply and generalized excess demand—are consistent with short-run economic contraction.

Keynesians emphasize the scenario in which supply exceeds demand. That is why Blinder characterizes short-run unemployment as a "demand-side" problem: If the economy is suffering from low employment and production, it must be because aggregate demand is "too low" relative to aggregate supply, requiring a cure in the form of government policies, for example, deficits that will boost aggregate demand.

An alternative view that emerged in the 1950s and then gathered steam in the 1970s observed that it is equally likely that aggregate demand could exceed aggregate supply, so that the appropriate policy response would be to reduce aggregate demand through, for example, government surpluses (Barro and Grossman 1974). This is often referred to as a case of "suppressed inflation," a name that comes from wartime experiences with price controls. As we go forward, we will see that the same phenomenon can result, not from price controls, but from a failure of the economy to generate wage and price increases needed to keep aggregate supply in line with aggregate demand.

Volume II shows how a suppressed inflation scenario could develop because of failure on the part of employers to raise wages in line with rising prices and from other factors that prevent wages from rising in tandem with prices as aggregate demand rises.

Once we admit the possibility of suppressed inflation, we have to consider the fact that a protracted downturn could be the result of too much, rather than too little, aggregate demand. There can be subnormal production and employment if either aggregate supply exceeds aggregate demand (as in the Keynesian scenario) or if aggregate demand exceeds aggregate supply (as in the suppressed inflation scenario).

A Revised View of the Long Run

This book focuses on macroeconomic policy and therefore gives attention both to policies that are effective in long-run "normal" times and to policies that are needed in short-run "abnormal" times. From the foregoing discussion it is clear that in order to conduct this inquiry, it will be necessary to distinguish between two very different "supply-side" problems. One stems from policies that prevent firms from using "inputs more efficiently" and the other from a supply shortfall brought about by the maladjustment of prices and wages.

When there is a failure of prices and wages to adjust and therefore a protracted downturn in the economy, there is a case for "nonclassical" solutions in the form of expansive or contractive monetary and fiscal policy, whichever may be called for. Then the need will be for a correct diagnosis of the problem (too little demand or too little supply) and the application of the appropriate remedies.

By looking at the problem in this manner, we undertake a radical departure from conventional books on macroeconomics. Macroeconomists traditionally take the approach adopted by Blinder in his 2003 *Wall Street Journal* article. In that approach there is only one diagnosis to perform, which is to answer the question whether the moment is right for a short-run or long-run remedies.

This book approaches the problem differently. We first (in Volume I) examine the economy under new classical assumptions (which is to say, in the long run) and consider the policies that cause distortions in the markets for labor and capital. We next (in Volume II) consider the possibility of a protracted downturn and whether nonclassical remedies in the form of expansive or contractive monetary and fiscal policy are called for.

In order to avoid terminological confusion, the book will recognize a distinction between two kinds of economic subperformance: (1) short-run (though, possibly protracted) subperformance brought about by imbalances between aggregate supply and demand and (2) long-run subperformance brought about distortions in the markets for labor and capital. In discussing the first kind of subperformance, we will distinguish between imbalances attributable to excess aggregate supply (the Keynesian scenario) and imbalances attributable to excess aggregate demand (the suppressed inflation scenario).

The Great Contraction of 2007 to 2009 appears to have resulted from a Keynesian-type reduction in aggregate demand. In Volume II, Chapter 5, we see evidence that the weakness of the ensuing recovery may be attributable to a failure on the part of government to adopt a sufficiently expansive policy response. Yet, the evidence is not unambiguous. Given the distortions in the price system created by safety-net measures that were implemented concurrently with the downturn, it is likely that the eagerness of government to cushion the effects of the downturn contributed to its severity. These competing explanations exemplify the difficulty policy makers encounter in their efforts to hit upon the correct response to an economic downturn.

The Purpose of This Book

In two opinion columns in the *Wall Street Journal,* published over the period December 2017 to January 2018, Alan Blinder unwittingly provided an example of why current-day macroeconomics does not provide a cogent guide to macroeconomic policy. President Trump had signed the Tax Cuts and Jobs Act on December 20, 2017. The Act provided for steep reductions in business taxes, along with some, more modest, reductions in individual taxes. It also, according to government forecasts, could be expected to add $1.7 trillion to the federal deficit over the next 10 years (Hall 2017).

"Dec. 2017," wrote Blinder in his December 2017 article, "should go down in political history as a day of infamy or absurdity, probably both."

Besides being highly regressive, said Blinder, the tax cuts mandated by the Act, "blow a large hole in the federal budget," a feature of the Act that should worry "most Americans" (Blinder 2017).

After several readers pointed out the apparent inconsistency between this argument and Blinder's 2003 article advocating federal deficits, Blinder published another column just a month later, defending his complaints about the Tax Cuts Act. The explanation, he said, lay in the difference between running deficits in a depressed economy (which characterized the U.S. economy during the Obama years) and running deficits in an economy that is at full employment (which characterized the U.S. economy at the end of 2017). Deficits of the former kind, argued Blinder, do good. It is deficits of the latter kind that do harm (Blinder 2018). The problem, as Blinder saw it, was that, whereas the Obama deficits were the intended cure for the recession under way at the time, the deficits resulting from the Tax Cuts Act were the unwanted by-product of the Act.

Blinder's arguments have a basis in economic theory. In later chapters, we will allow that there is an argument for deficits in times of economic contraction. But Blinder attempts to deceive the reader when he says that 2017 was the "wrong time" to increase the deficit. The purpose of the Act was to expand investment, not increase the deficit. That it also increases the deficit is collateral damage. Arguably, 2017 was the perfect time to increase the deficit if doing so was the price that had to be paid in order to cut taxes on business profits.

In Volume II, Chapter 2, we show that, in the long run, it is temporary increases in government spending, not deficits, that drive up interest rates in the long run. It is true that there is a growing risk of future U.S. deficits becoming unsustainable. A budget deal, put together by Republican and Democratic members of Congress in February 2018, could, according to one estimate, add another $1.7 trillion to the U.S. debt over the next 10 years—that, on top of the $1.7 trillion to be added by the Tax Cuts and Jobs Act. The 2018 addition to the debt was the price that the country had to pay in order to avoid a government shutdown.

The question is how it is possible to forge a coherent macroeconomic policy in the face of such cross-currents in economic policy advice. The country began the first year of the Trump administration with the economy still experiencing abnormally slow growth. Long before Trump took office, there was bipartisan agreement on the need for corporate tax reform. A fiscal commission, established by President Obama, issued a report in 2010 in which it wrote as follows:

> The corporate income tax, meanwhile, hurts America's ability to compete. On the one hand, statutory rates in the U.S. are significantly higher than the average for industrialized countries (even as revenue collection is low), and our method of taxing foreign income is outside the norm. The U.S. is one of the only industrialized countries with a hybrid system of taxing active foreign-source income. The current system puts U.S. corporations at a competitive disadvantage against their foreign competitors. A territorial tax system should be adopted to help put the U.S. system in line with other countries, leveling the playing field. Tax reform should lower tax rates, reduce the deficit, simplify the tax code, reduce the tax gap, and make America the best place to start a business and create jobs (NCFRR 2010).

The question for Blinder and other critics is just how the 2017 legislation could have been written to satisfy their concerns about deficits but also to provide a needed reduction in corporate taxes. Any cut in tax rates would have resulted in a loss of revenue, meaning that any cut, by Blinder's logic, should have been made in tandem with cuts in spending. It would be useful to know whether Blinder would have been willing to accept cuts in entitlement spending as a price worth paying to reduce business taxes.

Organization of the Book

First, a word of warning. This book is not going to be useful if the reader is unwilling to wade through some math and graphics. It is intended to be accessible to anyone who can remember his high-school algebra. Such calculus as there is appears in an appendix and in footnotes. Yet, the book is not light reading for train or air travel. Better, perhaps, to enjoy the movie than to tackle this book in a short flight. I hope, of course, that many readers will not be deterred and will wade through to the end.

Why all the math? The reason is that, without the math, the reader will, to be blunt, continue to be vulnerable to the great amount of folklore that continues to misinform just about everyone's understanding of the topic. The math notwithstanding, the book can serve as a principal or supplementary text for Intermediate and Master's level courses in macroeconomics.

The book is an update and expansion of the book that came out under the same title in 2015. This edition adds new chapters on government spending and on monetary and fiscal policy. It works through deficit spending in more detail. It traces the economy from the end of the Great Contraction to the present day. There is also new coverage of growth topics such as Robert Gordon's *Rise and Fall of American Growth*, Piketty's *Capital in the Twenty-First Century*, and Lawrence Summer's take on secular stagnation. Much of original microfoundations material is unchanged.

Volume I is mostly about microfoundations, which is to say the individual choice calculus from which macroeconomic activity emerges. That volume first works through the principal accounting relations that describe the macroeconomy (Chapter 2). It then takes on three topic areas: individual choices to work and save (Chapters 3 to 4), the supply and demand for labor and capital (Chapter 5), and economic growth (Chapter 6). It concludes by describing how taxes and government spending affect individual choices to work, save, and invest (Chapters 7 and 8).

Chapters 3 and 4 of Volume I lay out what might be considered the book's core theory. Chapter 3 lays out a two-period model in which the individual must solve two problems: how to divide his current time between leisure and work and how to divide his current income between consumption and saving. Chapter 4 elaborates on the second problem by generalizing the individual's choice calculus to incorporate a planning horizon of any length. Chapter 5 extends the analysis of Chapters 3 and 4 to model the supply and demand for labor and capital as the aggregation of individuals' choices. There we work out the conditions under which the suppliers of capital (savers) are coordinated with investors to bring about an equilibrium capital stock. Likewise, we work out the conditions under which workers are coordinated with employers to bring about an equilibrium level of employment.

Volume II is more along the lines of traditional macroeconomics. It starts out by delineating the two principal policy instruments available to the federal government for correcting sustained contractions of the macroeconomy: monetary policy (Chapter 1) and fiscal policy (Chapter 2). It then proceeds to identify the conditions under which the government can apply these two policy instruments in order to restore the economy to full employment (Chapters 3 and 4).

Chapter 3 shows how the failure of wages and prices to adjust to changing economic conditions can lead to either a brief or a protracted spell of low employment. It first examines the conditions under which the classical assumptions of Volume I apply, which is to say, conditions necessary for there to be equality between aggregate supply and demand. It then divides the analysis of inequality between aggregate supply and demand into two possibilities: self-correcting inequalities and inequalities that will be long lasting in the absence of corrective government policies. In addressing self-correcting inequalities, it considers instances in which an inequality stems from myopia on the part of workers, who temporarily misinterpret changes in aggregate demand as changes in localized demand. We then consider instances in which employers suffer from their own kind of myopia, which causes them, similarly, to misinterpret changes in aggregate demand as changes in localized demand.

In Chapter 3 we next consider the possibility of protracted spells of low employment brought about by maladjustments in wages and prices in response to changes in aggregate demand. We ask how government can apply monetary and fiscal policy to the correction of the resulting contraction in economic activity.

Chapter 4 extends the analysis to consider the problem government faces in diagnosing a fall in employment for its root cause. We consider the consequences of a misdiagnosis of a spell in which real GDP falls below potential real GDP.

Chapter 5 takes up the Great Contraction of 2007 to 2009. It shows how the policy response to that recession was arguably misguided.

Chapter 6 ties both volumes together to show what I have tried to explain about the drivers of the macroeconomy and about the government policies that can alleviate an economic downturn. I find much to criticize in the Federal Reserve's policy of targeting interest rates in carrying an expansionary policy regimen.

It is hoped that the reader of this book will come away from it with a solid understanding of the foundations of macroeconomic analysis and, from that understanding, acquire a more sophisticated appreciation of the role of monetary and fiscal policy in macroeconomic policy analysis. It is also hoped that he or she will gain an understanding of how economic systems can slump into a protracted downturn and how, in forging the appropriate policy response to that downturn, it is important to diagnose the cause correctly.

The book offers, as the title suggests, an integrative approach to its subject. Ever since Keynes, there has been tension between Keynesian and the pre-Keynesian classical elements of macroeconomic theory. The goal here is to integrate these elements into a more internally consistent approach to the subject matter. More specifically, the goal is to integrate the short-run and the long-run elements of macroeconomic activity and policy, so as to avoid the approach common to other books, which is to take the reader through a series of alternative, disjointed models that leave the reader puzzled about which model works best.

This is not at all to say that I have been able to create a window to the world through which all macroeconomic reality can be seen clearly. On the contrary, I close with the warning that the evidence may point to many, equally plausible explanations of economic activity and as many plausible government policy options. I can only hope that, with this book, I have provided a path toward a better understanding of those options.

CHAPTER 2

Macro Measures

There are numerous ways to assess the performance of the macroeconomy. Toward the beginning of each month, the U.S. Bureau of Labor Statistics provides estimates of what might be the most commonly cited measures of macroeconomic performance—the number of jobs created or lost and the unemployment rate for the preceding month. The attention given to these numbers reflects the Keynesian-inspired preoccupation with jobs or, more precisely, with the failure of the private sector to "create" enough jobs to eliminate the excess supply of labor brought about by a lack of aggregate demand.[1]

As fascinated as politicians and the public might be with the employment numbers, there is a more comprehensive measure issued every calendar quarter, which is the growth of real, inflation-adjusted gross domestic product during the preceding quarter. It is this indicator to which economists most often refer to in assessing macroeconomic performance.

Gross domestic product (GDP) is the market value of final goods and services produced within a country over a year's time. Even though it is the most commonly used measure of macroeconomic performance across the globe, GDP has come in for criticism in recent years as a macroeconomic indicator.

In his book, *Gross National Happiness,* Arthur C. Brooks claims that it is "happiness" that matters and that happiness has little to do with GDP, but depends more on the nation's commitment to spiritual and family values.

---

[1] It's a characteristic of this obsession to ignore the possibility that employment is lower than we might wish because there are too few workers who want to work. We will comment at length about this possibility in future chapters.

The astronomical rises in American GDP reflect the fact that, as a nation, we are creating huge amounts of value—we are the most successful nation on earth. Yet... happiness *doesn't* follow GDP growth over time. In the United States, our gross national happiness has remained essentially static for the past three decades. [(Brooks 2008, pp. 124–25 (emphasis original)].

In 2008, French president Nicholas Sarkozy commissioned a group of scholars to produce a report in which they would identify "the limits of GDP as an indicator of economic performance and social progress." A key finding was "that the time is ripe for our measurement system to *shift emphasis from measuring economic production to measuring people's well-being.*" The authors cite "an increasing gap between the information contained in aggregate GDP data and what counts for common people's well-being." Alternative measures of well-being include consumption and household income, household wealth, the distribution of income and wealth, and nonmarket services that households provide for themselves [(Stiglitz et al. 2010, pp. 1, 10–14), emphasis original].

Why GDP Still Matters

The book you are reading focuses on GDP and does so unashamedly. Yes, it is easy to cite examples of how GDP provides a misleading measure of economic performance and, indeed, happiness. The destruction of the World Trade Center added billions of dollars to GDP in the form of construction costs for the new tower. Automobile accidents increase GDP by requiring the services of ambulances, doctors, car repair shops, and lawyers. Hard as it is to believe, the royalties paid to rap performers add to GDP. Drug deals that take place in the underground economy go uncounted. But these anomalies do not undermine the importance of measuring economic activity that does take place and, as puzzling as it often seems, in response to consumer demand. There is no conflict between the policy of encouraging real GDP growth and that of discouraging terrorist attacks and traffic accidents, even while we tolerate loud, unpleasant noise masquerading as music.

The problem with critiques such as those offered by Brooks and by the Sarkozy Commission is that they make perfect sense without providing a useful alternative to GDP as a measure of economic performance. "Well-being is multidimensional," say that authors of the Sarkozy report (Stiglitz et al. 2010, p. 15). Well, yes, but that's just the problem. Once we expand the measurement of economic performance to encompass such indicators as "political voice and governance" and "social connections and relationships," any hope of identifying policy changes that rather clearly improve or worsen macroeconomic performance is lost. To muse about social connections is to drift off into speculations about matters best left to metaphysicians and social psychologists.

Henceforth, the emphasis here will therefore be on GDP. More specifically, the emphasis will be on what we call "real" GDP and its annual growth as reported by the Bureau of Economic Analysis (the BEA) of the U.S. Department of Commerce.

Before we delve into the component parts of GDP, let's understand the difference between "nominal" and "real" GDP. Nominal GDP is obtained either by (1) adding up the production that takes place within the country at final market prices or (2) adding up the incomes that are generated within the country in the course of the activities that give rise to this production. Real GDP is obtained by adjusting the nominal GDP for inflation.

Nominal Versus Real GDP

Let's consider a country in which two goods, A and B, are produced over a span of two years. Table 2.1 provides data on the quantity of each good produced and the price at which it is sold in each year. We see that $60.00 (= $1.00 × 60) worth of good A was produced in year 1 and $162.50 worth of the same good in year 2. Thus, in "nominal" dollars, production

Table 2.1 *Prices and Quantities, Years 1 and 2*

	Year 1	Year 2
Price ($) of good		
A	$1.00	$2.50
B	$2.00	$2.75
Quantity of good		
A	60	65
B	70	90

has increased by 171% from year 1 to year 2. But not all of this increase was "real." The number of units produced rose by only 8.3% (from 60 to 65). The rest of the increase in nominal output was due to inflation—the rise in price from $1.00 to $2.50. Similarly, production of good B, in nominal dollars, rose from $140.00 to $247.50. Part of this was real (the rise in output from 70 to 90 units) and part inflation (the rise in price from $2.00 to $2.75).

See Table 2.2. Row 1 provides calculations of nominal GDP (indicated by the Greek letter Ψ (psi, pronounced "sigh")), for each of the two years. Nominal GDP equals the market price of each good multiplied by the quantity produced and summed over all the goods.

Nominal GDP numbers are useful, but only insofar as we can divide them into their real and inflation components. The problem for the economists at the BEA is how to do this, given that both the prices and the mix of goods making up GDP change from year to year.

The BEA used to calculate real GDP by picking a base year and then using the prices in that year to weight quantities produced in subsequent years. This is called the "fixed weight" method, as illustrated in rows 3 and 4 of Table 2.2, where we provide calculations of real GDP, using year 1 as the base year. What this means is that we calculate real GDP for both years using current-year quantities but year-1 prices. Because year 1 is chosen as the base year, nominal and real GDP for year 1 are the same. But real GDP differs from nominal GDP for year 2, insofar as we use year-1 prices to calculate the former but year-2 prices to calculate the latter. In the parlance of national-income-and-product accounting, we use year-1 prices as weights for calculating real GDP.

At this point it is useful to mention that, in calculating real GDP, size matters only insofar as we need it to determine the growth of real GDP from one year to the next. Thus, using the FW(1) method, which uses year-1 prices as weights, we find that real GDP grew by 22.50% $\left(= \dfrac{\$245}{\$200} - 1 \right)$ from year 1 to year 2. See row 4, column 4.

The problem with this approach, quite obviously, is that it places too much weight on year-1 prices. The consequence is an exaggeration of the measured growth in real GDP. (Consider what it would mean to use ten-year-old prices in measuring the contribution to current GDP of smartphone

Table 2.2 *Calculating real GDP*

	1	2	3	4
			Year 1	Year 2	Growth of Real GDP
1	Ψ	$P_{A1}Q_{A1} + P_{B1}Q_{B1}$	$P_{A2}Q_{A2} + P_{B2}Q_{B2}$	
2		$\$1\times60 + \$2\times70 = \$200$	$\$2.50\times65 + \$2.75\times90 = \$410$	
3	Y (FW1)	$P_{A1}Q_{A1} + P_{B1}Q_{B1}$	$P_{A1}Q_{A2} + P_{B1}Q_{B2}$	
4		$\$1\times60 + \$2\times70 = \$200$	$\$1\times65 + \$2\times90 = \$245$	$\$245 / \$200 - 1 = 22.50\%$
5	Y (FW2)	$P_{A2}Q_{A1} + P_{B2}Q_{B1}$	$P_{A2}Q_{A2} + P_{B2}Q_{B2}$	
6		$\$2.50\times60 + \$2.75\times70 = \$342.50$	$\$2.50\times65 + \$2.75\times90 = \$410$	$\$410 / \$342.50 - 1 = 19.71\%$
7	$\dot{Y}$(CW)			$\sqrt{1.2250\times1.1971} - 1 = 21.10\%$
8	Y(CW)	$\$1\times60 + \$2\times70 = \$200$	$\$200(1 + 0.2110) = \$242.20$	

services, whose price, thanks to Walmart and other vendors, has gone down in recent years as the amount of those services used has dramatically risen.)

The current approach therefore is to use a "chain-weight" method under which the BEA annually updates both prices and quantities. To see how this works, examine rows 5 and 6, where, instead of using year 1 prices as fixed weights, we use year 2 prices. Now nominal and real GDP are the same for year 2, whereas real GDP for year 1 differs from nominal GDP for year 1 insofar as we use year 2 prices to calculate the former and year 1 prices the latter. Using this measure, the growth of real GDP is measured as 19.71% $\left(= \dfrac{\$410.00}{\$342.50} - 1 \right)$.

The chain-weight method integrates the FW-1 method and the FW-2 method into a single measure. This is the geometric mean of the growth of FW-1 GDP and of FW-2 GDP, which is calculated as shown in row 7. Using this method, real GDP grew by 21.10% $(= \sqrt{(1.2250 \times 1.1971)} - 1)$ from year 1 to year 2.

The BEA uses this method to calculate the growth of real GDP from year to year. Returning to Table 2.2, and letting year 1 be the base year, we see that real GDP in year 2 is now calculated as year-1 real GDP times one plus the chain-weight growth rate of real output.

$$Y = \$200 \times 1.2110 = \$242.20 \qquad (2.1)$$

In the National Income and Product Accounts (NIPA), the current base year is 2009. Thus, in Table 2.3, taken from the NIPA, nominal GDP (Ψ) and real GDP (Y), are shown as the same in 2009. In 2009, real GDP, Y, was \$14,419 billion. The chain-weight growth of real GDP ($\hat{Y}$), from 2009 to 2010, was 2.53%, so that real GDP in 2010 was \$14,784 billion (= \$14,419 billion $\times$ 1.0253).

We can now use this method to divide nominal GDP growth into components of real GDP growth and inflation. We begin with the formula

$$\Psi = PY, \qquad (2.2)$$

which is to say that nominal GDP equals the price level times real GDP. In 2010, P equaled 1.22% (before rounding). Applying this formula to 2010, we get

Table 2.3 U.S. GDP data (in $billion)

Year	Ψ	(%)	Y	(%)	P	(%)
2000	$10,285	NA	$12,560	NA	0.82	NA
2001	$10,622	3.28	$12,682	0.97	0.84	2.44
2002	$10,978	3.35	$12,909	1.79	0.85	1.19
2003	$11,511	4.86	$13,271	2.80	0.87	2.35
2004	$12,275	6.64	$13,774	3.79	0.89	2.30
2005	$13,094	6.67	$14,234	3.34	0.92	3.37
2006	$13,856	5.82	$14,614	2.67	0.95	3.26
2007	$14,448	4.27	$14,874	1.78	0.97	2.11
2008	$14,719	1.88	$14,830	−0.30	0.99	2.06
2009	$14,419	−2.04	$14,419	−2.77	1.00	1.01
2010	$14,964	3.78	$14,784	2.53	1.01	1.00
2011	$15,518	3.70	$15,021	1.60	1.03	1.98
2012	$16,155	4.10	$15,355	2.22	1.05	1.94
2013	$16,692	3.32	$15,612	1.67	1.07	1.90
2014	$17,428	4.41	$16,013	2.57	1.09	1.87
2015	$18,121	3.98	$16,472	2.87	1.10	0.92
2016	$18,625	2.78	$16,716	1.48	1.11	0.91

Source: U.S. Bureau of Economic Analysis (www.bea.gov).

$$\Psi_{2010} = 1.0122 \times \$14{,}784 \text{ billion} = \$14{,}964 \text{ billion.} \quad (2.3)$$

We can think of real output, Y, as nominal output, Ψ, divided by the price level, P.[2] Also the growth (percentage change) of nominal output, $\widehat{\psi}$, is the sum of the percentage change of P, denoted by $\widehat{P}$, and the percentage change of Y, denoted by $\widehat{Y}$:

$$\widehat{\psi} = \widehat{P} + \widehat{Y}. \text{ Thus} \quad (2.4)$$

$$\widehat{\psi}_{2010} = 1.00\% + 2.53\% \approx 3.53\%. \quad (2.5)$$

---

[2] P is called the "implicit price deflator" in the NIPA.

This is an approximation.[3] The exact number is

$$\hat{\psi}_{2010} = \frac{\psi_{2010}}{\psi_{2009}} - 1 = \frac{\$14,964\,\text{billion}}{\$14,419\,\text{billion}} - 1 = 3.78\%. \quad (2.6)$$

These formulas become important in subsequent chapters, in which we discuss the sources of real GDP growth and inflation.

The Components of GDP

The NIPA contain dozens of tables presented in bewildering detail to anyone brave enough to wade through them.[4] The good news is that, once these tables are boiled down to a few simple relationships, we have a powerful tool for grasping the policy issues that go to the heart of macroeconomic thought.

In a simplified model of the world, GDP can be thought of as a three-sided relationship. On the first side, we add up all the production that takes place as a result of domestic and foreign expenditures on goods produced in the home country. On the second side, we add up all the income to residents that is generated as a result of these expenditures, and on third side we account for all the ways residents use this income.

Table 2.4 breaks down GDP into its principal expenditure components. Personal consumption expenditures, (C) are purchases of goods and services by residents. Gross private domestic investment (I) equals spending on capital. I equals net private domestic investment plus consumption of private fixed capital or depreciation (D).

$$I = \text{Net } I + D = \$667 \text{ billion} + \$2,390 \text{ billion} = \$3,057 \text{ billion.} \quad (2.7)$$

Later we will think of Net I as the change in the capital stock, so that

$$I = \Delta K + D. \quad (2.8)$$

---

[3] This does not add up to 3.78% because of rounding and because of the way we compute percentage changes. The discrepancy would be smaller if we did not use rounded numbers and if we computed the percentage change using logarithms.

[4] Take a look at https://bea.gov/iTable/iTable.cfm?ReqID=9&step=1#reqid=9&step=1&isuri=1.

Table 2.4 Expenditure components of U.S. GDP (2016)

Component	$ billion	As a % of GDP
Gross domestic product (GDP)	18,625	100.00
Personal consumption expenditure (C)	12,821	68.84
+ Gross private domestic investment (I)	3,057	16.41
Net private domestic investment (Net I)	667	3.58
+ Consumption of private fixed capital (D)	2,390	12.83
+ Government purchases (G)	3,268	17.55
Government consumption expenditures (GC)	2,658	14.27
+ Gross government investment (GGI)	610	3.28
+ Net exports (NX)	−521	−2.80
Exports (X)	2,215	11.89
Imports (M)	2,736	−14.69

*All data are in nominal dollars. Some numbers in this and subsequent tables may not add up due to rounding.
Source: U.S. Bureau of Economic Analysis (www.bea.gov).

In the NIPA, both government and private firms engage in purchases of capital goods or investment. Private and government purchases of capital goods is called total capital spending. We have to include depreciation when calculating capital spending since a portion of that spending goes to replace depreciated capital. Only the remaining portion can be counted as net investment.

Net exports (NX) are exports minus imports, where exports (X) are goods and services bought by foreign residents from home country producers, and imports (M) are goods and services bought by home country residents from foreign country producers:

$$NX = X - M = \$2{,}215 \text{ billion} - \$2{,}736 \text{ billion} = \$ -521 \text{ billion.} \quad (2.9)$$

Government consumption expenditures consist of compensation paid to government employees and purchases of intermediate goods and services. Government gross investment is government spending on structures and equipment. We designate the sum of government consumption expenditures and government gross investment as *G*:

$$G = GC + GGI = \$2{,}658 \text{ billion} + \$610 \text{ billion} = \$3{,}268 \text{ billion.} \quad (2.10)$$

Government purchases (*G*) are not to be confused with government expenditures, which include spending funds that the government simply takes from taxpayers and provides to recipients, without any provision of goods and services in exchange. These funds are identified in Table 2.5 as government transfer payments (G*TR*), which are mainly social benefits distributed to U.S. residents, interest payments on government debt (*INT*) and government subsidies (*SUB*). It is notable that 57% of current government spending goes for transfer payments, interest on the debt, and subsidies.

Usually when we think of the government deficit, it is just the difference between government spending and government revenues. For example, in FY 2016, overall U.S. government spending was $3,853 billion and revenue from all sources was $3,268 billion, with a deficit of $585 billion.

The NIPA, however, distinguish between government's current spending and government's capital spending, where current spending is for government consumption, transfer payments, interest payments, and subsidies. Government consumption is for the salaries of government employees and other current items. Government capital spending, called "gross government investment," is for structures and equipment.

Thus, in NIPA parlance, it is the "net government saving" on current account that measures the deficit. See Table 2.5. There, we see that government current expenditures exceed current income by $865 billion, for a net saving of –$865 billion or a deficit of $865 billion.

We can measure GDP in terms of its expenditure components. Using Ψ, again, to stand for nominal GDP, we get

$$\Psi = C + I + G + NX = \$12,821 \text{ billion} + \$3,057 \text{ billion}$$
$$+ \$3,268 \text{ billion} - \$521 \text{ billion} = \$18,625 \text{ billion}. \qquad (2.11)$$

Now let's approach the calculation of nominal GDP, which we continue to designate as Ψ, from the income, as opposed to the expenditure, side of the ledger. See Tables 2.5, 2.6 and 2.7.

Gross domestic product measures production that takes place within the home country. Gross national product (GNP) measures production by home country residents. The difference is net receipts of factor income from the rest of the world (*NRFI*) (see Table 2.5).

Table 2.5 The government current account (2016 in $billion)

Net government saving (NGS)	−865
Total government income (TGINC)	5,313
Tax revenue (TR)	4,980
+ Other government income (OGINC)	333
− Total government current expenditures (TGEXP)	6,178
Government consumption expenditures (GC)	2,658
+ Transfer payments (GTR)	2,786
+ Interest payments (INT)	672
+ Subsidies (SUB)	62

Source: U.S. Bureau of Economic Analysis (www.bea.gov).

Table 2.6 GNP and National income (2016, in $billion)

Gross national product (GNP)	18,822
Gross domestic product (GDP)	18,625
+ Net Receipts of Factor Income from the Rest of the World (NRFI)	197
Net national product (NNP)	15,905
Gross national product (GNP)	18,822
− Consumption of fixed capital (CFC)	2,917
Consumption of private fixed capital (D)	2,390
+ Government consumption of fixed capital (GFC)	526
National Income (NI)	16,052
Net national product (NNP)	15,905
− Statistical discrepancy (STAT)	−147

Source: U.S. Bureau of Economic Analysis (www.bea.gov).

Table 2.7 Sources of National income (2016, in $billion)

National Income	16,052
Compensation of employees (WAGES)	9,979
+Proprietors' income (PROP)	1,342
+Rental income (RENT)	707
+Corporate profits (CORP)	2,074
+Net Interest (NINT)	571
+Taxes on production and imports less subsidies (PROT)	1,288
+ Business transfer payments (BTR)	164
− Subsidies (SUB)	62
+ Surplus of government enterprise (SUR)	−10

Source: U.S. Bureau of Economic Analysis (www.bea.gov).

$$\text{GNP} = \text{GDP} + \textit{NRFI} = \$18,625 \text{ billion} + \$197 \text{ billion}$$
$$= \$18,822 \text{ billion}. \hspace{3cm} (2.12)$$

GNP and GDP differ insofar as some home country production provides income to foreigners and some foreign production provides income to Americans. Thus, income earned by Germans from Volkswagens produced in the United States is part of U.S. GDP but not U.S. GNP. Income earned by Americans on Apple products produced in China are part of U.S. GNP but not U.S. GDP.

Net national product (NNP) is GNP minus depreciation (consumption) of fixed capital. National income (see Table 2.6) equals NNP except for a statistical discrepancy between the measured value of total production and the measured value of total income generated by production. National income consists of (1) income received by businesses and persons for supplying the services of labor and capital for production, (2) taxes on production and imports, and (3) adjustments for transfer payments made by business to persons, government, and the rest of the world (BTR), for subsidies to business (SUB), and for the current surplus on government enterprises (SUR). See Table 2.7.

Personal income is income received by persons, as opposed to businesses. The BEA calculates personal income as compensation paid to employees plus profits, rent, asset income, and transfer payments received by persons minus "contributions" for governmental social insurance (principally Social Security and Medicare taxes).[5] Disposable personal income equals personal income minus personal taxes and certain nontax payments and is disposed of in the form of consumption, personal saving, interest payments, and personal transfer payments. See Table 2.8.

In the Keynesian model, there is an important issue concerning the disposition of disposable personal income between consumption and personal saving. This is because, in that model, saving is considered a

---

[5] The BEA continues the tradition of calling Social Security taxes "contributions," as if the taxpayer voluntarily contributes his money in exchange for a promise of future benefits. In fact, these payments are taxes in exactly the same manner as income taxes are taxes, and they carry with them no enforceable promise of future benefits.

Table 2.8 Personal income and disposable personal income (2016, in $billion)

Personal Income (*PIN*)	15,929
Compensation of employees (*WAGES*)	9,979
+ Proprietors' income (*PROFITS*)	1,342
+Rental Income of persons (*RENT*)	707
+Personal income receipts on assets (*ASSETINC*)	2,378
+Personal Current Transfer receipts (*TR*)	2,768
– Contributions for government social insurance (*SS*)	1,245
Disposable personal income (*DPI*)	13,969
Personal income (*PIN*)	15,929
– Personal Taxes (*PT*)	1,960

Source: U.S. Bureau of Economic Analysis (www.bea.gov).

"leakage" from the economy. Table 2.9 breaks down disposable personal income in terms of its disposition between consumption, saving, and other items.

Just as we obtained GDP earlier by adding up its expenditure components, we can also obtain GDP by adding up the various ways that the incomes are generated in producing goods and services. As Table 2.6 shows, the BEA arrives at the national income by adjusting GDP for *NRFI* and depreciation (consumption) of fixed capital. Personal income, which is income going to persons rather than businesses, equals factor payments to persons plus transfer payments to persons minus contributions for Social Security and other social insurance programs, as detailed in Table 2.8. Disposable personal income is personal income after personal taxes (mainly personal income taxes).

People make use of their disposable personal income by engaging in consumption, paying interest on credit cards and on personal loans, making transfer payments (e.g., charitable contributions) to other persons, and engaging in personal saving (Table 2.9).

Let's look a little more deeply in to the calculation of personal income. Both businesses and persons receive income for producing goods and services. The problem is that there is no airtight distinction between the two entities. About 46% of corporate profits are distributed to persons as dividends. But corporations are owned by persons (shareholders, including

Table 2.9 Disposition of disposable personal income (2016, in $billion)

Disposable personal income (DPI)	13,969
Personal consumption expenditures (C)	12,821
+ Personal Interest Payments (PINT)	278
+ Personal transfer payments (PTP)	189
+ Personal Saving (PS)	681

Source: U.S. Bureau of Economic Analysis (www.bea.gov).

institutions), so the remaining portion is at least indirectly received by persons too. Corporations pay interest to individual corporate bond holders out of corporate revenues. Unincorporated entities like single proprietors pay individual income taxes on their profits.

The BEA derives personal income by first subtracting corporate income from national income and then adding back in that portion of their income that corporations distribute to persons as dividends and interest payment.

Now let's reverse the process in order to show how we can arrive at national income by starting with personal income. As one step in this process, we need to calculate an item that we will call T, which stands for "taxes minus personal receipts of government transfer payments." Think of T as the net impact of government taxes and cash benefits on persons. Table 2.10 provides details.

To find national income, let's then itemize all the ways in which persons dispose of their income, as shown in Table 2.9. Next add T, and then calculate the business income that is not counted as part of personal income and subtract corporate taxes. We will call this $BIMCT$. We then get:

$$NI = C + PINT + PTP + PS + T + BIMCT = \$12,821 \text{ billion}$$
$$+ \$278 \text{ billion} + \$189 \text{ billion} + \$681 \text{ billion}$$
$$+ \$2,122 \text{ billion} - \$39 \text{ billion} = \$16,052 \text{ billion}. \qquad (2.13)$$

That gets us to Table 2.11. Note that C, PS, and T make up 97% of national income. We can therefore simplify the accounting, and with no harm to the analysis, if we treat every item in equation (2.13) and

Table 2.10 Calculation of T (2016, in $billion)

Taxes minus personal receipts of government transfer payments (T)	2,122
Personal taxes (PT)	1,960
+ Contributions for government's social insurance (SS)	1,245
+Taxes on production and imports less subsidies (PROT)	1,226
+ Corporate taxes (CORPT)	459
– Personal transfer receipts from government (TR)	2,768

Source: U.S. Bureau of Economic Analysis (www.bea.gov).

Table 2.11 Disposition of National income (2016, in $billion)

National Income (NI)	16,052
+ Personal Consumption expenditures (C)	12,821
+ Personal Interest Payments (PINT)	278
+ Personal Transfer Payments (PTP)	189
+ Personal Saving (PS)	681
+ Taxes on income and production minus government transfers to persons (T)	2,122
+ BIMCT	–39

Source: U.S. Bureau of Economic Analysis (www.bea.gov).

Table 2.11 except *C*, *PS*, and *T* as being equal to zero. We therefore, in effect, assume that business income not passed on to persons consists only of corporate taxes. We also ignore interest that persons pay on their credit cards and charitable contributions and transfer payments that persons make to each other.

Now let's move on to saving. Table 2.12 breaks down saving into its components. Gross saving is the sum of gross private saving (*S*), net government saving (*NGS*), and depreciation of government capital (*GFC*). Gross private saving is the sum of net private saving (*NPS*) and consumption of private fixed capital, or depreciation (*CFC*).

Now we can simplify further. If we treat all government spending as current spending, then *GFC* is zero and *CFC* in Tables 2.6 and 2.12 becomes *D*. Next, if we assume that all private saving is personal saving, then *NPS* = *PS*, and we end up with a new, simplified formula for national income:

Table 2.12 Gross saving and its components (2016, in $billion)

Gross Saving (GS)	3,353
Gross Private Saving (S)	3,692
Net Private saving (NPS)	1,301
Business Saving (BS)	621
+ Personal Saving (PS)	681
+Consumption of private fixed capital (CFC)	2,391
+ Net government saving (NGS)	–865
+ Government consumption of fixed capital (GFC)	526

Source: U.S. Bureau of Economic Analysis (www.bea.gov).

$$NI = C + PS + T. \qquad (2.14)$$

Now return to Table 2.6. We can make a few more assumptions that will further simplify our task. First, we can set $NRFI$ and $STAT$ equal to zero. Then:

$$GDP = NI + D. \qquad (2.15)$$

which means that

$$GDP = C + PS + T + D. \qquad (2.16)$$

Or, because $PS + D$ now equals S,

$$GDP = C + S + T. \qquad (2.17)$$

One further simplification remains to be done. The BEA reports data for an item that it calls "net lending or net borrowing." This item used to be called "net foreign investment" (NFI), defined as "the net acquisition of foreign assets by U.S. residents less the net acquisition of U.S. assets by foreign residents." Because the expression net foreign investment is more descriptive of what this item represents, I use it here: When Americans acquire foreign assets, they acquire claims on foreigners. When foreigners acquire American assets, they acquire claims on Americans. This is not really net lending, since many of the claims being acquired are not loans at all but the acquisition of equity in business located abroad.

When we combine net foreign investment with gross private domestic investment, gross government investment, and statistical discrepancy, we get gross investment (see Table 2.13), which just equals gross saving (Table 2.12):

$$GI = I + GGI + NFI + STAT = \$3,057 \text{ billion} + \$610 \text{ billion}$$
$$- \$461 \text{ billion} + \$147 \text{ billion} = \$3,353 \text{ billion.} \qquad (2.18)$$

Gross private domestic investment (I), can be expressed as the sum of private fixed private investment (FI) and changes in inventories, which we label ΔINV, so that

$$I = FI + \Delta INV = \$3,022 \text{ billion} + \$35 \text{ billion} = \$3,057. \quad (2.19)$$

We can then write:

$$GDP = C + FI + \Delta INV + G + X - M. \qquad (2.20)$$

This equation reminds us that GDP measures production, whereas C, FI, and G measure expenditures. If expenditures result in the sales of goods out of existing inventories, ΔINV is negative, which means

Table 2.13 *Gross investment and its components (2016 in $billion)*

Gross Investment (GI)	3,353
Gross Private Domestic Investment (I)	3,057
Private fixed investment (FI)	3,022
+ Change in inventories (ΔINV)	35
+ Gross government investment (GGI)	610
+ Net foreign investment (NFI)	−461
Net exports (NX)	−521
+ Net receipts of factor income from the rest of the world (NRFI)	197
+ Net Taxes and transfer payments from foreigners (TPF)	−137
− STAT	−147

Source: U.S. Bureau of Economic Analysis (www.bea.gov).

inventories fall by the amount sold out of inventories. This amount must be subtracted from expenditures in order not to overstate GDP. Similarly, insofar as residents spend money on imports, then imports must also be subtracted. If, conversely, expenditures don't keep up with production, ΔINV is positive. ΔINV must be added to expenditures in order not to understate production.

Next, we need to consider the balance on current account. This equals the difference between outlays by Americans to the rest of the world minus rest-of-the world outlays to Americans (see Table 2.14).

If we add net exports to net receipts of factor income from the rest of the world and subtract taxes and transfer payments to foreigners we get the balance on current account, which is just equal to net foreign investment. If, as is the case, Americans are spending more on imports and other items than foreigners are spending on Americans, then the current account must be in deficit and foreign claims on Americans must be rising faster than American claims on foreigners. Then also NFI must be negative.

We can calculate NFI as

$$NFI = NX + NRFI - TPF = -\$521 \text{ billion} + \$197 \text{ billion}$$
$$- \$137 \text{ billion} = -\$461 \text{ billion}. \qquad (2.21)$$

Note that NFI can also be calculated as:

$$NFI = GS - I - GGI + STAT = \$3{,}353 - \$3{,}057$$
$$- \$610 - \$147 = -\$461 \qquad (2.22)$$

Table 2.14 Balance on current account (2016, in $billion)

Balance on current account	−461
Net Exports (NX)	−521
Exports (X)	2,215
− Imports (M)	2,736
+ Net receipts of factor income from the rest of the world (NRFI)	197
+ Net taxes and transfers from foreigners (TPF)	−137

Source: U.S. Bureau of Economic Analysis (www.bea.gov).

As we go forward, we will ignore *NRFI* and *TPF*. Thus, we will define net foreign investment in terms of net exports:

$$NFI = NX. \qquad (2.23)$$

We can also define *NFI* as the sum of gross private saving and government saving minus gross private domestic investment:

$$NFI = S + (T - G) - I. \qquad (2.24)$$

The important lesson here is that our trade "imbalance" (the excess of imports over exports) can be explained as the excess of capital spending over national saving. This is an important reminder to those who see the U.S. trade deficit as a problem. One might equally well describe the "problem" as an excess of U.S. capital spending over saving. If the goal is to reduce the trade deficit, then the goal also is to find some way to increase private saving, reduce the government deficit, and reduce domestic investment.

Here are a few examples of how net exports translate into net foreign investment:

Example 1
- French wine sellers have a bank account of $2,000 in Kansas on January 1, 2018.
- In 2018, Kansans import $1,000 worth of wine from France and export $500 worth of soybeans.
- At end of 2018, the French wine sellers have $2,500 in their account (because they added $1,000 by selling wine and subtracted $500 by buying soybeans).
- The change in U.S. claims on foreigners is zero and the change in foreign claims on the United States is $500.
- *NFI* = $0 – $500 = –$500. *NX* = $500 – $1,000 = –$500.

Example 2
- French wine sellers have a bank account of $2,000 in Kansas on January 1, 2018, and Kansas soybean sellers have a bank account in Paris of $2,000 worth of Euros.

- In 2018, Kansans import $1,000 worth of wine from France and export $500 worth of soybeans.
- At end of 2018, the French wine sellers have $3,000 in their bank account in Kansas (because they sold $1,000 worth of wine) and Kansans have $2,500 worth of Euros in their bank account in Paris (because they sold $500 worth of soybeans).
- The change in U.S. claims on foreigners is $500 and the change in foreign claims on the United States is $1,000.
- $NFI = \$500 - \$1,000 = -\$500$, $NX = \$500 - \$1,000 = -\$500$.

Example 3

- French wine sellers have a bank account of $2,000 in Kansas on January 1, 2018, and Kansas soybean sellers have a bank account in Paris of $2,000 worth of Euros.
- In 2018, Kansans import $1,000 worth of wine from France and export $500 worth of soybeans.
- The French also spend $1,000,000 opening up a vineyard in Kansas. The American manager of the vineyard imports $1,000,000 worth of equipment from France. So now U.S. exports = $500 and imports = $1,001,000.
- Just as in Example 2, the French wine sellers have $3,000 in their bank account in Kansas at the end of 2018 (because they sold $1,000 worth of wine) and Kansans have $2,500 worth of Euros in their bank account in Paris (because they sold $500 worth of soybeans). The French also now own a U.S. facility, which is worth $1,000,000.
- The change in U.S. claims on foreigners is $500 and the change in foreign claims on the United States is $1,001,000.
- $NFI = \$500 - \$1,001,000 = -\$1,000,500$. $NX = \$500 - \$1,001,000 = -\$1,000,500$.

Now some final simplifications are in order. We will henceforth assume that the income side of GDP has just three components, *LAY* (labor income), *NW* (nonwage income), and *D*, where *NW = PROFITS + RENT + ASSET INC.*

This permits us to write

$$\text{GDP} = LAY + NW + D \qquad (2.25)$$

and

$$\text{GDP} = C + I + G + NX = C + S + T = LAY + NW + D. \quad (2.26)$$

This simplified algebra will prove useful as we proceed with the analysis.

CHAPTER 3

Individual Equilibrium

The title of this chapter might seem puzzling to the reader. In Chapter 1, we distinguished macroeconomics from microeconomics by defining the former as applying to aggregate economic activity and the latter to individual economic activity.

Yet, macroeconomic activity boils down to decisions to supply labor and financial capital (which is what people provide when they save) to firms that use their labor and financial capital to produce the goods that workers buy. This means that we have go through some microeconomics before aggregating the choices made at the microlevel to the entire economy.

So let's start with some fundamentals: Firms produce things because individuals are willing to supply them with labor and financial capital. People supply labor because the reward for doing so, as measured by their after-tax earnings, exceeds the reward for not doing so, as measured by forgone pleasures of leisure and as affected by the numerous incentives government offers to people not to work.

People save because the after-tax return they receive for putting their cash into financial instruments like bank certificates of deposits (CDs) and corporate stocks exceeds the pleasures of using that cash for current consumption. Their incentives to save are, as we shall see, diminished by taxes on capital income.

This chapter and the next will work through the details of what determines people's willingness to work and save. Once we have the groundwork in place for determining how people choose to work and save, we will then consider how firms take their work and saving and convert it into production.

Why Am I Writing This Book?

At any moment, I have a choice between working and not working. At this moment I am writing the book in front of you. In the parlance of economics, I am sacrificing leisure and, in the process, supplying labor services in exchange for what I hope to be the income (and satisfaction) that I will enjoy several months from this moment when the book is published. Maybe I will apply the future income I get from writing the book toward the purchase of a car. Or maybe I will use it to acquire financial assets that I will need to fund my eventual retirement. In the first instance, and on the basis of narrow pecuniary considerations, I would use the income to finance current consumption and, in the second, again in the parlance of economics, to finance future consumption or leisure.

Suppose, on the other hand, that instead of writing this book, I were engaged in a consulting project for which I was paid as I worked. The consulting assignment would pay a fixed, agreed-upon amount immediately, not a royalty contingent on book sales. So which is the better choice? The book or the consulting project?

The fact is that either pursuit—the book or the consulting project—would require the sacrifice of current leisure so that I might as well choose the project (the book) from which I would get more personal satisfaction, no matter what pecuniary reward I might get. Thus the choice of the book-writing project became the superior one in my personal calculus.

Yet, I did perform a cost-benefit test before committing to it. It was a matter of making choices at the margin: the sacrifice of some certainty and an immediacy of rewards in exchange for personal satisfaction and the hope that the future rewards from the book will exceed the current rewards from any other use of my time.

I make these reflections, not because I think they will fascinate the reader, but because of how obvious they must seem, once revealed. Every person in every day of his or her life makes choices like the one I did. You might ask yourself: Shall I double down at the office and work all the harder in hopes of a promotion, or shall I take the time to polish my resume and start looking for something better? Shall I take a part-time job now that the kids are in high school and make the needed investment in new clothes and maybe a new car, or shall I go back to school or just stay at home until they are in college?

The government presents us with other less appealing choices. Shall I take another job and boost my income or just let well enough alone and avoid disqualifying my family from health care subsidies or unemployment insurance? Shall I take the higher paying job on the other coast or avoid uprooting my family and pushing us into a higher tax bracket? Shall I save more now or believe the government's promises about future Social Security benefits? How about that stock tip from my broker? Should I buy the stock or not, considering that the tax on corporate income has just gone down, or just put the money in a low-paying but safe CD?

Such choices, as they are made every day by every participant in the economic system, give rise to the activity we study under the heading of macroeconomics. Yes, when we assess or predict the performance of the "macroeconomy," we look at broad indices of how individual choices combine to produce overall economic activity, but behind those indices are minute choices of the kind just described in which people make trade-offs between the different uses of their time and money.

Macroeconomists, as noted in the Introduction, look at the big trade-offs, and not the small ones. We look at the total number of hours available to the age-eligible population and think about how that population divides those hours between work and leisure. We look at national income and think about how the country divides what's left of that income after taxes between consumption and saving. We think big.

But we also think small. That's because, as noted before, all the big choices are the result of small choices by individuals about how to divide their time between work and leisure and how to divide their after-tax income between consumption and saving. Thus we have to drill down to the choice calculus of the individual who must decide how to spend each day as it looms ahead of him at 5:00 a.m. (I'm an early riser) and how to use each paycheck that appears (minus the part that goes to government) each month in his bank statement.

That is the way macroeconomists of the new classical persuasion approach their subject, and that is the way we approach macroeconomics in this chapter.

Oh, and one more thing. This chapter and the next embrace what macroeconomists call a *microfoundations* approach: working up to the big from the small. A characteristic of this approach is that it makes use of a hypothetical individual called the "representative agent." In this book, to avoid worrying my editors in an age of gender sensitivity, I have two representative agents: Adam and Eve. I rely on Biblical authority to start with Adam, but after he has been expelled from Eden and faces the necessity of making worldly trade-offs.

So let's begin with the problem faced by Adam when it comes to supplying his labor services. There are 24 hours in a day, 168 hours in a week, and 8,760 hours in a year. Adam, whom we assume to be 16 or older and not in prison (i.e., a member of the age-eligible population), must spend every one of those hours either working for money or not working for money. Economists, as previously stated, characterize this as a choice between work and leisure even if time counted as leisure includes going to college, cutting the lawn, or any other activity, however pleasurable or onerous, that is not directed at making money. (We ignore barter as offering the option of gains from trade without the need for money.)

The reader may think it strange to imagine a worker carefully deciding every day, week, or year how much time to allocate between work and leisure. Shall Adam work eight hours today? Or six? Or 16? Twelve months this year or only three? In fact, there are many occupations that provide flexibility in choosing working hours. And there are workers with eight-hour-a-day jobs who choose to work part time at other jobs. And many workers move in and out of eight-hour-a-day and temporary jobs over the course of their lifetimes.

In deciding how to divide his time between work and leisure, Adam has to take into account how his current choices will affect his future choices. If he makes $100 by working an hour today, he could spend the entire amount today or use the $100 to buy some income-earning asset and then use the cash value of that asset to engage in consumption at a later time. Or he could enjoy leisure and put off work to the future.

The Labor—Leisure Choice

Let's suppose that Adam has just two periods to live: period 1 and period 2. Period 1 starts on a given day at midnight and period 2 is the day that begins a year later at midnight. (It is as if, Adam comes back to life in a year, in a manner reminiscent of Rip Van Winkle.) The period-1 wage rate is w_1, and the period-2 wage rate is w_2. In period 1, Adam has h

hours available to divide between leisure and labor. (Because we will usually think in terms of the labor-leisure choice over a single day, h is taken
to equal 24.) Let's abbreviate period-1 labor income as lay_1 (This follows
the convention of using the letter y to designate income, in this instance
labor income, and lower-case letters to represent individual rather than
societal choices.) Then

$$lay_1 = w_1\left(h - le_1\right), \tag{3.1}$$

where le_1 is the amount time Adam allocates to leisure in period 1, so that
if $le_1 = 16$, he works eight hours that day. (There are no taxes to worry
about just yet. We postpone that worry to future chapters.)

We can write a similar equation for lay_2, his period-2 labor income:

$$lay_2 = w_2\left(h - le_2\right). \tag{3.2}$$

Adam can receive income in the form of wages (sometimes called
"earned income") or in the form of income on some asset that he owns,
such as a bank CD ("unearned income" or asset income). For now let's
assume that Adam's total period-1 income y_1 is labor income, so that

$$y_1 = lay_1, \tag{3.3}$$

but that he can receive asset income as well as labor income in period 2.
Adam can receive a return of r on an asset that he purchases out of his
saving sav_1 in period 1. He then divides his period-1 income between
consumption c_1 and saving sav_1, so that

$$sav_1 = lay_1 - c_1. \tag{3.4}$$

Now we can write an equation for his total income in period-2 as

$$y_2 = lay_2 + sav_1\left(1 + r\right). \tag{3.5}$$

Note that y_2 has three parts: (a) Adam's period-2 labor income, lay_2,
his period-2 interest income, $r \times sav_1$, and his income, sav_1, from the sale

of the asset he bought in period 1. In this thought experiment, we have to imagine that Adam thinks in terms of how his saving on May 1, 2018, will contribute to his income on May 1, 2019.

So far, because labor income depends on the division of time between labor and leisure, Adam has three variables, le_1, le_2, and sav_1, for which to solve in order to determine his total income in period 1 and period 2.

Substituting equation (3.4) into equation (3.5), we get

$$y_2 = lay_2 + (lay_1 - c_1)(1+r). \qquad (3.6)$$

Because the individual thinks only in terms of the two periods, we assume that he will not save in period 2. Thus that part of his period-2 consumption that is affected by his period-1 choices will be equal to his period-2 labor income plus however much he saved in period 1 plus the return on his saving. Think of Adam as buying an IOU in period 1 for which he pays sav_1 and then sells the IOU just before it matures in period 2 for $sav_1(1 + r)$. That becomes his income from saving. His period-2 consumption then is

$$c_2 = lay_2 + (lay_1 - c_1)(1+r). \qquad (3.7)$$

Rearranging,

$$c_1 + \frac{c_2}{1+r} = lay_1 + \frac{lay_2}{1+r}. \qquad (3.8)$$

The left-hand side of this equation represents the present value of Adam's current and future consumption and the right-hand side the present value of his current and future labor income. The equation illustrates the principle that at every moment in our lives we are making a choice between current and future consumption based on expectations about our current and future income. To understand this, let's get a firm idea of what is meant by "present value."

Suppose that $r = 10\%$, $lay_1 = \$500$, and $lay_2 = \$550$. Then the present value of Adam's labor income is $1,000. The present value of lay_1 is $500 because that is the money that he will receive during the current period.

The present value of the \$550 to be received a year from now is, at 10% interest, also \$500 $\left(= \dfrac{\$550}{1+0.1} \right)$.

To see what this means, suppose that Adam wants to spend \$1,000 in period 1. He has only \$500 in income in that period, so in order to spend \$1,000 in period 1, he must borrow against his period-2 labor income. Because the interest rate is 10%, he would have to borrow \$500 now and pay back principal and interest of \$550 out of his period-2 income. If he takes this route, he is left with no money to apply to consumption in period 2. Or Adam could, at the other extreme, consume nothing in period 1, put his period-1 income in the bank, so that with interest he would have \$550 to apply to his period-2 consumption, permitting him to set his period-2 consumption at \$1,100.

Now let's rewrite equation (3.8) as follows:

$$lay_1 = c_1 + \frac{c_2 - lay_2}{1+r}. \tag{3.9}$$

This tells us that labor income in period 1 can be used to finance period-1 consumption or period-2 consumption, or to reduce period-2 labor income and thus period-2 work time. Conversely, period-2 labor income can be used to finance period-1 consumption or period-2 consumption, or to reduce period-1 labor income and thus period-1 work time. Everything depends on everything else.

But how does Adam make these trade-offs? Let's approach this question by assuming for now that, in choosing lay_1, Adam takes lay_2 as fixed and that in choosing lay_2 he takes lay_1 as fixed. (We will relax that assumption later on.)

We also need some assumptions about how Adam chooses between labor income and leisure. Most fundamentally, we assume that Adam wants to maximize utility. In Chapter 4 we will discuss the idea of maximizing the present value of a *utility function*, which is defined over consumption that takes place for an entire lifetime. Here we keep things simple by sticking with the two-period example.

Let's first think of our decision-maker Adam as having to choose between more or less leisure now. Suppose Adam has been dividing his day between 10 hours of work and 14 hours of leisure and that he has been making \$500 per day in income. Now he considers expanding his leisure by one hour. The question is how much income, at most, would he be willing to sacrifice for that additional hour of leisure?

In considering a problem like this we can imagine that Adam carries a computer around in his head, which assigns units of utility—*utiles*—to different quantities of things. This brain computer assigns a certain number of utiles to Adam's leisure time and certain number to his income. For now, we don't have to care about Adam's *total utility* from leisure and income. All we have to care about is his *marginal utility* of leisure and of labor income. The marginal utility of leisure is the change in utility that Adam experiences per unit change in leisure, which can be written as $\frac{\Delta U}{\Delta le}$. Suppose, for example, that an additional hour of leisure would increase Adam's utility by 400 utiles. Then we would write:

$$\frac{\Delta U}{\Delta le} = \frac{400}{1} = 400, \tag{3.10}$$

which is to say that the change in Adam's utility per unit change in leisure is 400. We see Adam choosing leisure time in terms of hours. So one more hour of leisure adds 400 to Adam's total utility.

Now let's ask about the marginal utility of his labor income. Let's suppose that the following equation applies:

$$\frac{\Delta U}{\Delta lay} = \frac{4}{1} = 4, \tag{3.11}$$

which means that the change in his utility per unit change in labor income is 4. One more dollar of labor income adds 4 units of utility. Labor income adds to utility because it makes it possible to consume more, now or later.

Proceeding with this example, the question is how much income, at most, would Adam be willing to give up for an additional hour of leisure? The answer is $100. Why? To show why (if it isn't already obvious) we introduce another concept, which we will call the *marginal rate of substitution of leisure for labor income* (MRS_{LeLay}). We can define the MRS_{LeLay} as

$$MRS_{LeLay} = \frac{\Delta U / \Delta le}{\Delta U / \Delta lay} = -\frac{\Delta lay}{\Delta le}, \tag{3.12}$$

which indicates the amount of labor income the individual is willing to give up for another unit of leisure or, equivalently, the amount of labor income with which the individual must be compensated to be willing to give up a unit of leisure. In this example, the MRS_{LeLay} is $100 $\left(= \dfrac{\$400}{4}\right)$.[1]

We assume that utility rises with a rise in both leisure and income, so that the individual always prefers more leisure to less leisure and more income to less income. Thus, in Figure 3.1, where we measure Adam's leisure along the horizontal axis and his labor income along the vertical axis, he prefers the combination of leisure and labor income indicated by point X to that indicated by point Y_1 and that to point Z.

Just as Adam always prefers more to less, in this fashion, he can be indifferent between combinations like Y_1 and Y_2, where one combination has more income than the other, but less leisure, or more leisure but less income. A curve that traces out these combinations is called an *indifference*

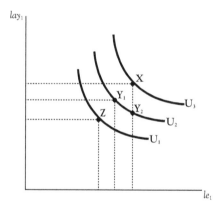

Figure 3.1 Individual indifference curves for leisure and labor income

---

[1] A clarification about signs: In calculating the MRS_{LeLay}, we assume either that labor income rises as leisure falls or that labor income falls as leisure rises. Thus $\frac{\Delta lay}{\Delta le}$ must be negative. Because we want to think of MRS_{LeLay} as a positive number, we thus place a minus sign in front of $\frac{\Delta lay}{\Delta le}$ to get MRS_{LeLay}. We follow this convention throughout the book.

curve, and it indicates different combinations of leisure and labor income that register a fixed amount of utility in Adam's brain computer.

Figure 3.1 contains three such indifference curves, all of which have some properties in common: (1) they are negatively sloped, to reflect the idea that for Adam to remain at the same level of utility, he has to give up some leisure as income expands, (2) they do not intersect (which is necessary for his choices to be consistent), and (3) they are bulged downward, that is, "convex." Adam's total utility rises as he moves from indifference curve U_1 to indifference curve U_2 to indifference curve U_3 but constant as he moves along any of these curves.

Now our job is to lay out a process by which Adam makes his leisure-work choices in period 1. We begin by assuming that work becomes more onerous, and leisure more desirable as more and more time is allocated to work. A person who is working 14 hours a day, and has only 10 hours a day for sleep and other "leisure" activities, would be willing to give up quite a bit of labor income for another hour of leisure, whereas a person who is working four hours a day, and already has 20 hours of leisure, would be willing to give up only a little labor income for an extra hour of leisure. Hence, the downward bulge in the indifference curves. Let's illustrate, beginning with the same example we just considered.

See Figure 3.2. If Adam is at point X_1 on one of his indifference curves, he is consuming 10 hours of leisure and getting $700 per day in income. Now he considers expanding his leisure from 10 to 11 hours, so that he

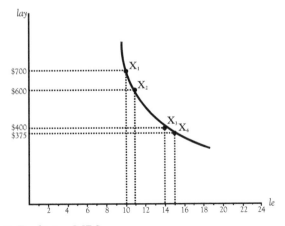

Figure 3.2 **Declining MRS**$_{LeLay}$

would move from point X_1 to point X_2. We see that he can sacrifice as much as $100 in income in making this move without moving to a lower level of utility. Now compare a possible move from X_3 to X_4. Once Adam has expanded his leisure time to 14 hours per day, he is willing to give up only as much as $25 in labor income for another hour of leisure.

Adam's MRS_{LeLay} is $100 when he has 10 hours a day in leisure and $25 when he has 14 hours a day in leisure. His choices are governed by the law of *diminishing marginal rate of substitution of leisure for labor income*, whereby the amount of labor income he is willing to give up for an hour of leisure falls as leisure increases. Equivalently, the amount of labor income with which he must be compensated in order to give up an hour of leisure decreases as his leisure expands.

Figure 3.3 shows how Adam picks the combination of consumption and leisure that maximizes his utility, that is, leaves him in the best position. Here we assume that he gets a wage of $50 per hour, as measured by the slope of the line CD, and that he has to decide how to allocate his time each day between consumption and leisure. If he wanted to, he could (technically at least) have either (1) $1,200 in labor income and no leisure or (2) no labor income and 24 hours of leisure or any linear combination in between.

In this example, Adam picks point X_2 where he makes $500 in wages, allocating 10 hours of his day to work and 14 hours to leisure. Why X_2? The answer is that any other point on CD would leave him worse off.

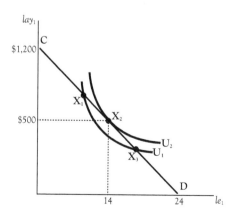

Figure 3.3 Individual equilibrium in the leisure and income choice calculus

First, Adam will not pick points X_1 or X_3 because they lie on an indifference curve U_1, which lies below the indifference curve U_2 on which X_2 is located. We can see this also if we measure the marginal rate of substitution as the absolute value of the slope of the indifference curve, wherever we find ourselves along an indifference curve on line CD.[2] We would expect indifference curves to be steep for combinations of leisure and labor income that contain a small amount of leisure and large amount of labor income and to be flat for combinations that contain a large amount of leisure and a small amount of labor income. Thus, the indifference curve for U_1 is steeper at point X_1 on CD than it is at X_3.

At point X_1, Adam is willing to give up more than $50 in labor income for another unit of leisure, as measured by the slope of indifference curve U_1 at that point. Because it costs only $50 in foregone wages and consumption for an additional unit of leisure, he will increase utility by moving down CD toward point X_2.

At points to the right of X_2, Adam is willing to give up less than $50 in labor income for an additional hour of leisure. At point X_3, for example, the last hour of leisure enjoyed was worth less than $50, as evidenced by the flatness of the curve. Adam will want to move back up CD to point X_2. Thus the optimal choice of consumption and leisure is represented by point X_2. It is at this point that the slope of his highest attainable indifference curve U_2 is just equal to the slope of line CD, which equals $50. Because, at this point,

$$MRS_{LeLay} = w = \$50, \qquad (3.13)$$

Adam cannot increase his utility by either reducing or increasing the amount of leisure he enjoys.

Now let's examine Adam's period-2 calculus and in combination with his period-1 calculus just described. We represent this in Figure 3.4. Panel

---

[2] Absolute value means numerical value. The slope of a downward sloping line is negative, but it is more convenient to speak in terms of the numerical value (say, 100) of the slope, rather than the actual value of the slope (say, −100). To make the language less cumbersome, we will often talk about the "slope" of an indifference curve even though we really mean the absolute or numerical value of the slope.

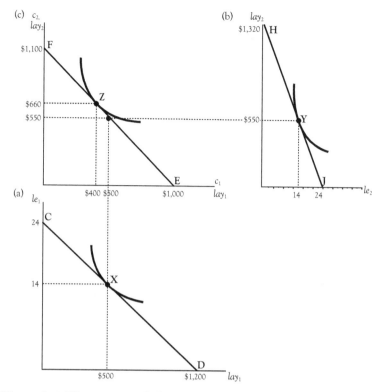

Figure 3.4 The two-period choice calculus

(a) presents the same information as Figure 3.3, except that the vertical axis is now the leisure axis and the horizontal axis is the labor income axis. (By flipping the axes in this figure, we can observe the combined results of his period-1 and period-2 choices.) Panel (b) illustrates Adam's period-2 choices, with the horizontal axis serving as the leisure axis and the vertical axis as the labor income axis, as before. We assume that he expects his period-2 wage rate to be $55 per hour. Adam (coincidentally) chooses to allocate 10 hours to work and 14 hours to leisure in both period 1 and period 2. His period-2 labor income is $550. In equilibrium,

$$MRS_{LeLay} = w = \$55. \tag{3.14}$$

Panel (c) illustrates the choice faced by Adam in choosing between period-1 and period-2 consumption. Assume that there is an interest rate of 10%, which Adam receives on any money he saves and which he pays on any money he borrows. He can then have as much as $1,000 in period-1 consumption, and $0 in period-2 consumption, if he wishes, or $0 in period-1 consumption and $1,100 in period-2 consumption or any linear combination of these choices.

The Consumption—Saving Choice

Let's see how these choices present themselves. We have already seen how Adam could end up with $1,000 in period-1 consumption and $0 in period-2 consumption. In this event, he simply consumes all of his period-1 income, which comes to $500. Then he borrows money from the bank (or maybe his trusting brother-in-law) for $500, promising to pay $500 plus interest of $50 when the loan comes due. That will leave him with $1,000 to consume in period 1 but nothing to consume in period 2. We can think of this as a process in which Adam sells an IOU to a lender and then pays off the IOU a year later.

Alternatively, Adam could use all of the $500 of current income to buy an IOU and then, when the IOU comes due in a year, supplement his period-2 labor income with the $550 principal and interest from the IOU to finance $1,100 in consumption. Line FE in Figure 3.5 illustrates these and all the intermediate possibilities. As in our earlier example, the present value of Adam's period-1 and period-2 labor income is $1,000:

$$PV = lay_1^* + \frac{lay_2^*}{1+r} = \$500 + \frac{\$550}{1+0.1} = \$1,000, \qquad (3.15)$$

where lay_1^* indicates the equilibrium choice of labor income in period 1, and lay_2^* indicates the equilibrium choice of labor income in period 2.

The future worth of Adam's period-1 and period-2 labor income is $1,100:

$$FW = lay_1^*(1+r) + lay_2^* = \$500(1+0.1) + \$550 = \$1,100. \quad (3.16)$$

The slope of FE equals 1.1, reflecting the fact that Adam foregoes $1.10 [= $1(1 + r)] in consumption in the next period for each $1 he puts into consumption in this period. We say that the opportunity cost

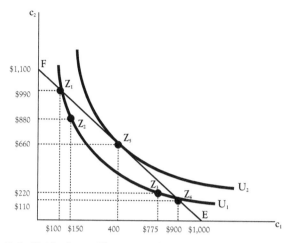

Figure 3.5 Individual equilibrium in the two-period consumption model

of $1 in consumption in this period is $1.10 in consumption in the next period.

Adam has a utility-maximization problem in having to choose between current and future consumption. A dollar allocated to current consumption is a dollar not saved and a dollar not saved is a dollar plus earnings that is unavailable for future consumption. So the question is how the utility gained by adding a dollar to current consumption compares to the utility foregone by virtue of the resulting loss of future consumption. Let's write the marginal utility of period-1 and period-2 consumption as follows:

$$MU_{c_1} = \frac{\Delta U_1}{\Delta c_1} \text{ and} \tag{3.17}$$

$$MU_{c_2} = \frac{\Delta U_2}{\Delta c_2}, \tag{3.18}$$

where $\frac{\Delta U_1}{\Delta c_1}$ is the change in period-1 utility per dollar change in period-1 consumption, and $\frac{\Delta U_2}{\Delta c_2}$ is the change in period-2 utility per dollar change in period-2 consumption.

Part of the answer to the question just posed lies in the size of these variables: Insofar as the marginal utility of period-2 consumption exceeds the marginal utility of period-1 consumption, the individual is advised to shift consumption from period 1 to period 2.

Another consideration has to do with how Adam weighs period-2 utility against period-1 utility. We assume that he always puts the higher weight on current, or here, period-1 utility, than on future, or period-2, utility. We use ρ (the Greek letter rho) to indicate the amount of period-2 utility with which Adam must be compensated in order to willingly give up a unit of period-1 utility. We call ρ his *rate of time preference*. Thus the present value of period-1 plus period-2 utility is

$$PVU = U_1(c_1) + \frac{U_2(c_2)}{1+\rho}, \qquad (3.19)$$

which, in plain English, means that the value now of Adam's current utility combined with his future utility is his current utility plus his future utility discounted by his rate of time preference. Then his marginal rate of substitution of current for future consumption is

$$MRS_{c_1 c_2} = \frac{MU_{c_1}}{MU_{c_2}}(1+\rho). \qquad (3.20)$$

Suppose that Adam's period-1 utility rises by 200 utiles if he gets another dollar of period 1 consumption so that

$$MU_{c_1} = 200, \qquad (3.21)$$

and suppose that his period-2 utility rises by 105 utiles if he gets another dollar of period-2 consumption, so that

$$MU_{c_2} = 105. \qquad (3.22)$$

Finally suppose that his rate of time preference is 5%, meaning that, for Adam, a utile now is worth 5% more than a utile later.

This permits us to think about how the present value of Adam's utility changes with his period-1 and period-2 consumption. The change in the present value of his marginal utility per unit change in period-1 consumption is

$$\Delta PVU / \Delta c_1 = MUc_1(1+\rho) = 210. \qquad (3.23)$$

And the change in the present value of his marginal utility per unit change in period-2 consumption is

$$\Delta PVU \, / \, \Delta c_2 = MU_{c_2} = 105. \qquad (3.24)$$

Then the marginal rate of substitution of c_1 for c_2 is

$$MRS_{c_1 c_2} = \frac{\Delta PVU \, / \, \Delta c_1}{\Delta PVU \, / \, \Delta c_2} = \frac{MU_{c_1}(1+\rho)}{MU_{c_2}} = \frac{210}{105} = 2. \qquad (3.25)$$

Adam is willing to give up \$2 of period-2 consumption for \$1 of period-1 consumption.

In Figure 3.5 we represent Adam's preferences with indifference curves that have the same properties as the indifference curves presented in Figures 3.1 and 3.2. Each indifference curve reflects a higher level of utility than the indifference curves below it. Each has the familiar downward slope and a convex shape. And each has a property similar to the indifference curves just considered in examining the choice between leisure and labor income. This property is the *diminishing marginal rate of substitution of period-1 consumption for period-2 consumption.*

Line FE in the diagram represents the choices before Adam, given that he has \$1,000 that he could spend now and given that he could have \$1.10 in future consumption for every dollar that he saves now, which implies that $r = 10\%$. Alternatively, we can say that Adam gives up \$1.10 in period-2 consumption for every dollar he allocates to period-1 consumption.

Thus, if Adam spent the entire \$1,000, he would have nothing to spend in period 2. If he spent only \$100 now and saved the remaining \$900, he would have \$990 to spend in period 2, and so forth.

Suppose Adam chooses point Z_1, where his period-2 consumption would be \$990, and considers expanding his period-1 consumption from \$100 to \$150. We see, from curve U_1, that he would remain at the same level of satisfaction if he reduced his period-2 consumption to \$880 and shifted to point Z_2. There he would consume \$150 worth of goods in period 1 and \$880 in period 2. We can calculate his marginal rate of substitution of period-1 for period-2 consumption approximately as

$$MRS_{c_1 c_2} = -\frac{\Delta c_2}{\Delta c_1} = -\frac{\$880 - \$990}{\$150 - \$100} = 2.20. \qquad (3.26)$$

Adam is willing to give up, on the average, $2.20 of period-2 consumption for another dollar of period-1 consumption as he shifts from Z_1 to Z_2. But he has to give up only $1.10 in period-2 consumption in order to add another dollar to his period-1 consumption. Knowing this, he would want to expand his period-1 consumption. As he keeps expanding his period-1 consumption he would be willing to give up less and less of period-2 consumption for an extra dollar of period-1 consumption.

Now suppose Adam moves from Z_2 to Z_3. At Z_3, he consumes $775 in period 1 and $220 in period 2. His marginal rate of substitution is now approximately 1.06 (=$660/$625). He has expanded his period-1 consumption too far if he adjusts to point Z_3, in that he was willing to sacrifice, on average, adjusting from point Z_2 to point Z_3 only $1.06 of future consumption for another dollar of current consumption, whereas again, every dollar of current consumption that he enjoys costs him $1.10 in future consumption. The mistake grows worse if he shifts all the way to Z_4, in that the marginal rate of substitution has fallen still further and now equals 0.88 (=$110/$125). He was willing to give up only $0.88 in future consumption for another dollar of present consumption, whereas the future cost of that dollar of present consumption was, again, $1.10. He would want to move up line FE, expanding his period-2 consumption and contracting his period-1 consumption.

Adam can adjust to any point he wishes along the line FE but chooses the point that permits him to attain the highest indifference curve with a point in common with that line. As before, we can measure the $MRS_{c_1 c_2}$ at any point along an indifference curve by finding the slope of the indifference curve at that point. We see that he would maximize utility by adjusting to point Z_5, where the slope of curve U_2 just equals the slope of FE. There his marginal rate of substitution also just equals $1 + r = 1.10$.

The concept of diminishing $MRS_{c_1 c_2}$ is important for the discussion in Chapter 5 of capital formation. The $MRS_{c_1 c_2}$ equals the amount of future consumption the individual is willing to forego for another dollar of current consumption. As the individual expands current consumption and thus decreases current saving, the amount of future consumption he is willing to forego for another dollar of current consumption declines. But the $MRS_{c_1 c_2}$ can also be interpreted as the amount of future consumption with which the individual must be compensated in order to forego another dollar of current consumption. The other side of the coin is that the $MRS_{c_1 c_2}$ rises as current consumption decreases and current saving rises.

This means that a business that seeks financial capital in order to engage in investment must offer a high enough reward to induce the saving needed to provide that financial capital. When Adam saves, he creates financial capital. He does that if he puts his saving in the bank, so that the bank can lend to a customer, or if he buys stock in a corporation. He even creates financial capital if he puts his saving in a cookie jar, perhaps as a buffer against future emergencies.

Putting the Choices Together

Now return to Figure 3.4. As mentioned previously, Adam's period-1 wage rate is $50. See panel (a). His period-2 wage rate is $55, as shown in panel (b). The decision to have 14 hours of daily leisure in both period 1 and period 2 translates into $500 in period-1 labor income and $550 in period-2 labor income. The decision to have $400 in period-1 consumption then translates into a decision to have $660 in period-2 consumption: Our decision maker, Adam, consumes $400 of his $500 in period-1 labor income, saving $100. He then augments his period-2 consumption with $110 in spending, as he cashes in the asset that he bought for $100 in period 1, which is now, at 10% interest, worth $110. In this way, he can set his period-2 consumption at $660.

Figure 3.6 illustrates how a change in the wage rates for period-1 and period-2 can affect these choices. In panel (a), Adam's period-1 wage rate has risen from $50 to $70. In panel (b), his period-2 wage rate has fallen from $55 to $50. Period-1 leisure falls from 14 to 12 hours and thus work expands from 10 to 12 hours. Conversely, the fall in his period-2 wage rate causes him to expand leisure from 14 to 16 hours and to contract work from 10 to 8 hours.

In panel (c), the budget line FE, imported from Figure 3.4, correspondingly shifts outward in a manner parallel to itself so that it now

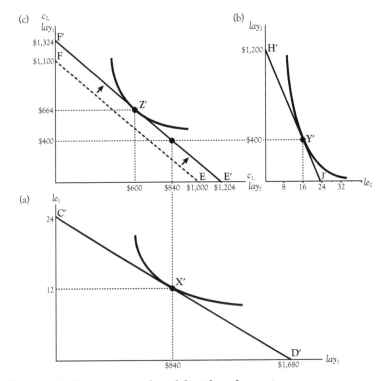

Figure 3.6 The two-period model with a change in wage rates

becomes line F'E', intersecting the horizontal axis at $1,204 and the vertical axis at $1,324. We determine this by computing

$$PV = lay_1^{*'} + \frac{lay_2^{*'}}{1+r} = \$840 + \frac{\$400}{1+0.1} = \$1,204, \text{ and} \qquad (3.27)$$

$$FW = lay_1^{*'}(1+r) + lay_2^{*'} = \$840(1+0.1) + \$400 = \$1,324. \qquad (3.28)$$

Adam decides to set his period-1 consumption at $600 and his period-2 consumption at $664.

We can take a policy lesson away from this demonstration. In the Keynesian model, to be examined in Volume II, Chapter 3, current consumption equals some fixed fraction of disposable income, and saving is the residual that is left over after spending. The role of government in determining consumption (and saving) derives from its power to raise or lower disposable income through the exercise of monetary and fiscal policy.

In this chapter, the individual decides what fraction of his income to allocate to consumption on the basis of the comparative utility of consumption now versus consumption later. The role of government is to determine how its policies affect this decision, given that its policies, in particular its tax policies, affect the reward for saving and therefore the funds that are available to finance capital spending. Our task, later, will be to consider which model better fits current economic circumstances.

Returning to our model, another possibility is that r would change. See Figure 3.7. There we replicate Figure 3.4, except that the interest rate rises to 15%. The effect of the higher interest rate is seen in the rotation of the budget line from FE to F'E'. Now, because the interest rate and, therefore the cost of borrowing, is higher, the individual finds that the maximum amount Adam can allocate to current consumption falls from $1,000 to $978. By the same token, the maximum amount he could allocate to future consumption rises from $1,100 to $1,125. In this example, period-1 consumption falls from $400 to $300, and period-2 consumption rises from $660 to $780.

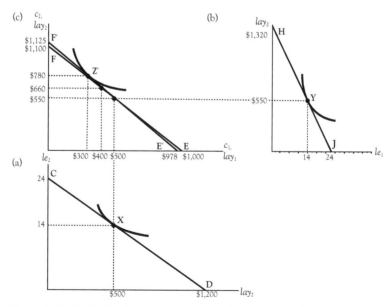

Figure 3.7 A rise in the interest rate in the two-period model

The Work-Now/Work-Later Choice

Next consider how Adam's work-leisure calculus would take into account not just the wage rate he gets now but also the return on his saving and the wage rate he might get in the future. It is intuitively clear that a high return to current saving will induce people to work more now. If Adam believes that the stock market will head straight up for the next few years but may not thereafter, he would have reason to work hard now so that he can save now and enjoy the fruits of his efforts later when the market goes down. Likewise, if Adam realizes that he is in his prime earning years, he will want to work hard now in order to save up for the years to come when his earning power will be diminished. Think about athletes who figure that they have until age 40 to make the big money and scientific geniuses who are convinced that they must make their score before they turn 30, after which their mental capacities will never again be so keen. This is as opposed to piano soloists and some college professors who keep going until they drop.

To simplify the problem, let's suppose Adam figures that he can make $50 an hour today but $25 an hour a year from now. Put differently, the cost of leisure for him now is twice what it will be in a year. Adam has an incentive to work especially long hours now, given that the reward for working will fall by 50% next year.

Suppose further that Adam can get 10% interest on a CD that will mature in one year. If he puts the $50 he makes by working an additional hour into the purchase of that CD, he will have $55 to spend next year. Now fast forward to next year, when he collects that $55 on the matured CD. With that much money, he can "buy" himself 2.2 (= $55/$25) hours of leisure: He does this by using the CD to replace the income he would lose by reducing his work time by 2.2 hours.

This tells us that the sacrifice entailed by taking another hour of leisure now can be seen in either of two ways: First, and as we have already seen, it entails the sacrifice of current income and therefore current and/or future consumption. Second, and alternatively, it entails the sacrifice of future leisure. The cost to Adam of another hour of leisure now is the 2.2 hours of leisure that he would have to sacrifice next year because of the labor and asset income that he sacrifices by taking that hour of leisure now. We can also say that if he gives up an hour of leisure today, he could reward himself with 2.2 more hours next year. Would it be in Adam's interest to give up that hour of leisure now? As usual, we need to do some math to tackle this issue.

Let the *marginal rate of substitution of current for future leisure* ($MRS_{Le_1 Le_2}$) be the amount of leisure Adam would give up in period 2 for another hour in period 1. Let's refer to period-1 leisure as current leisure and period-2 leisure as future leisure. In this example, he has to give up 2.2 hours of future leisure for another hour of current leisure. Suppose (1) that the $MRS_{Le_1 Le_2}$ = 2.5, meaning that he would be willing to give up 2.5 hours of future leisure for another hour of current leisure. Because it costs only 2.2 hours of future leisure to have another hour of current leisure, he will want to expand current leisure and contract future leisure.

Now suppose (2) that Adam's $MRS_{Le_1 Le_2}$ is 1.5, so that he is willing to give up only 1.5 hours of future leisure for another hour of current leisure, whereas it costs him 2.2 hours of future leisure for another hour of current leisure. In that instance, he would have expanded his period-1 leisure too far and would want to contract current leisure and expand future leisure.

Only when the amount of future leisure that Adam is willing to sacrifice for another hour of current leisure just equals the amount of future leisure that he must sacrifice for that additional hour of current leisure has he adjusted his work-leisure choices for both periods optimally. Formally, we write that Adam should adjust those choices so that

$$MRS_{Le_1 Le_2} = \frac{w_1(1+r)}{w_2}. \qquad (2.29)$$

The cost of another hour of current leisure is $\frac{w_1(1+r)}{w_2}$, which is to say, the amount of future leisure Adam must sacrifice in order to have that additional hour of current leisure. Adam will want to adjust his choices of leisure in both periods in such a way as to bring the value he places on current leisure, as measured by the value of $MRS_{Le_1 Le_2}$, into line with this cost.

Let's think about what this means to the macroeconomy. Suppose, in the forgoing example, that Adam has adjusted his allocation of leisure time between the two periods in such a way that he has satisfied equation (2.29):

$$MRS_{Le_1 Le_2} = \frac{\$50(1+0.1)}{\$25} = 2.2 \tag{3.30}$$

Now suddenly Adam's period-1 wage rate rises from $50 to $90.91 while his period-2 wage rate and his $MRS_{Le_1 Le_2}$ remain unchanged. Temporarily now

$$MRS_{Le_1 Le_2} < \frac{\$90.91(1+0.1)}{\$25} = 4. \tag{3.31}$$

the price of current leisure has risen from 2.2 to 4 hours of future leisure. Adam has an incentive to contract current leisure and expand future leisure. That is to say, he would want to expand current work and contract future work.

Alternatively, suppose that r rose from 10 to 15%, while the wage rate and his $MRS_{Le_1 Le_2}$ remain unchanged. Here again, the cost of current leisure would rise. Now he would face the following situation:

$$MRS_{Le_1 Le_2} < \frac{\$50(1+0.15)}{\$25} = 2.3. \tag{3.32}$$

Here again, there is an incentive to contract current leisure and expand current work, inasmuch as the cost of an hour of current leisure has risen from 2.2 to 2.3 hours of future leisure.

In this process, we encounter another version of the familiar idea of diminishing marginal rate of substitution. If Adam is in equilibrium to begin with and $\frac{w_1(1+r)}{w_2}$ falls, he will want to bring his $MRS_{Le_1 Le_2}$ back into line with $\frac{w_1(1+r)}{w_2}$ by expanding current leisure and contracting future leisure, through which process his $MRS_{Le_1 Le_2}$ will fall until it equals $\frac{w_1(1+r)}{w_2}$.

On the other hand, if, and as in the forgoing examples, he is in equilibrium to begin with and $\frac{w_1(1+r)}{w_2}$ rises, he will want to substitute future leisure for current leisure until his $MRS_{Le_1 Le_2}$ rises to equal $\frac{w_1(1+r)}{w_2}$.

The analysis so far provides some hints about the effects of government policy changes on individual behavior. We have seen, for example, that, acting rationally, people have an incentive to spread the effects of changes in current income over their future and present consumption. We will see that this is important in thinking through such matters as the burden of government debt on future generations and the effects of government policy changes on asset income.

Also, insofar as government can influence the wages that a person earns, policies that have the effect of increasing take-home pay (i.e., wages minus income and payroll taxes) can induce people to work more, just as policies that reduce take-home pay can induce them to work less. Our examples in Figures 3.4 and 3.6 showed as much, anyway. Finally, policies that cause a rise in the return to financial assets can induce people to work more and to save more.

It turns out, however, that things are not so simple. To see why, we have to recognize the distinction between substitution and income effects.

Substitution Versus Income Effects

Let's consider the scenario illustrated by Figure 3.8. Adam is initially at point X on line AB, where he receives a wage of $50 per hour and chooses 14 hours of leisure (hence, 10 hours of work) and $500 in labor income. Then his boss raises his wage from $50 to $100 per hour, putting Adam on line BC, where he chooses to work 12 hours and earn $1,200.

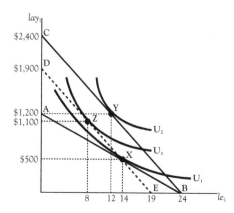

Figure 3.8 Separating substitution and income effects

We need to see how this rise in the wage rate exerts a *substitution effect* and an *income effect* on Adam's leisure-income choice. Before the wage rate rose, the *opportunity cost* to Adam of each additional hour of leisure was $50. Because that cost has now risen to $100, Adam will have an incentive to substitute work for leisure. The substitution effect occurs as a result of this change in the opportunity cost of leisure. The individual will always expand work at the expense of leisure when his wage rate rises, if we ignore the fact that the higher wage rate also makes him richer. But because it does make him richer, it also exerts an income effect that works in just the opposite way of the substitution effect.

In Figure 3.8, we see how it is possible to separate these two effects. Recall that Adam, hard worker that he is, decided to increase his work day from 10 to 12 hours, that is, to reduce his leisure from 14 to 12 hours. This takes him from point X to point Y. Now an economist comes along and suggests an experiment to Adam's boss. Under the experiment, his boss will tell Adam that the higher wage is still available but only if Adam agrees to contribute $500 a day to the boss's favorite charity. This puts Adam on line DE. Now Adam finds that if he were to return to point X and continue working the same 10 hours that he did before his wage was increased, his take-home pay would be only as high as it was before, which is to say, $500. By working 10 hours, he would earn $1,000 but, by being forced to give away $500 of that amount, he would be back to bringing home only $500.

However, Adam will not return to point X. Because the opportunity cost of leisure has risen and because he is now $500 poorer than he would have been had he not been forced to give away $500, he would shift to some point on DE such as Z, where he would work something more than 10 hours a day. In this example, he decides to work 16 hours a day (reducing his leisure to eight hours a day) and makes $1,600 before having to pay the $500 to the charity, leaving him with $1,100 in take-home pay.

Eventually, in this scenario, the experiment ends. Adam's boss says that Adam no longer has to give up $500 of his earnings and Adam is allowed to return to point Y, where he lives happily ever after. The purpose of this experiment was to isolate the substitution effect from the income effect of the wage change. The substitution effect was the adjustment from X to Z and the income effect was the adjustment from Z to Y.

Stripped of the income effect, Adam expands his work by six hours. With the income effect, he expands it by only two hours. The reason why the income effect causes him to reallocate two of those hours back to leisure is that leisure is desirable and becomes more affordable at a higher wage.

This demonstration reminds us that as wage rates rise, we should expect the quality of life to rise, not just because higher wage rates increase people's spending power but also because they permit people to allocate more time to leisure. Even if the individual ends up working more, as here, he has the option of working less while maintaining his standard of living.

Let's see how a rise in the wage rate affects the supply of labor. Figure 3.9 traces the effects of the preceding experiment on Adam's supply of labor. When the wage rate is $50, Adam is at point *A* and supplies 10 units of a labor. When the wage rate rises to $100, he increases his supply of labor to 12 (point *B*) or 16 (point *C*) units depending on whether the income effect is present or not. Figure 3.9 shows that there are two labor supply curves along which Adam could adjust—one that includes the income effect and one that includes only the substitution effect.

The alert reader will see that, if the income effect were large enough, Adam could actually reduce the quantity of labor he offers to his employer when his wage goes up. Yes, the substitution effect would induce him to provide more labor, but if the income effect is large enough it might overwhelm the substitution effect and he might, in the end, supply less labor.

This possibility comes up in discussions about tax policy. We will delve more deeply into tax policy in a later chapter, but we can see the

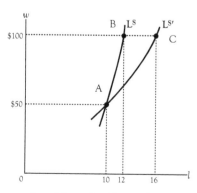

Figure 3.9 Labor supply with and without the income effect

outline of the problem now. "Supply-side" economists argue that if government taxes labor income at a lower rate, people will work more because their after-tax wage will rise and when they work more, the economy will expand as more labor enters production. But what if the income effect dominates and people respond to the increase in their take-home pay by working less rather than more?

One answer is that it shouldn't matter how they respond. A rise in take-home pay is welfare-enhancing whether the person whose pay rises enjoys benefits in the form of increased pay or increased leisure. Much of human progress is measured by the opportunities for leisure and the reduced onerousness of work that has come with technical progress and capital accumulation.

Income effects are also present when there is a rise in the return to saving (r in our examples). We go into this matter in much greater depth in the next chapter. But for now, look back at Figure 3.7, where we let an increase in r bring about a rise in saving. That same increase in r could, however, have also led to a decrease in saving as Adam took advantage of the higher r to increase current consumption. An increase in r increases the cost of current leisure but it also makes current consumption more affordable. We begin the next chapter with a consideration of the income effect of a change in r.

Policy Implications

While some might see these distinctions as nuances, they, in fact, have great importance in forging macroeconomic policy. A principal goal of macroeconomic policy is to increase work and saving (even though leisure and present consumption are good things, too). This goal derives its appeal from the fact that production is good and that it occurs because of the application of labor and capital to production. In order to get more production, some combination of the following must occur:

1. People must save more and investors must apply the increased saving to capital formation.
2. Workers must supply more labor and employers must apply the labor supplied to their capital.

3. Technology must advance.
4. Governmental and societal barriers to production, such as they are, must be reduced.

These are the timeless and everywhere-applicable conditions for increased production. This chapter had to do with items 1 and 2. Insofar as people want to save more as the return to saving rises and insofar as workers want to work more as wage rates rise *and* insofar as government can affect these variables, we see an opportunity for government to expand output.

This chapter was about the individual choices that drive the decision to supply labor and to save. For all the minutiae through which we had to wade, we covered only half the story on the matter of saving and work. The other half of the story concerns what must be true so that investors will want to apply saving to capital formation and so that employers will want to hire the labor supplied to them.

So what have we learned so far? Actually, two important things. First, increases in wage rates will increase the amount of labor people will want to supply, provided any income effect exerted along the way is less than the substitution effect. Second, increases in the return to saving increase saving provided, again, that any income effect is less than the substitution effect. Thus if the goal is to increase the supply of labor and to increase saving *and* if conditions are suitable, then government should adopt policies that cancel out the income effect. We will consider just what sorts of policies might do that in Volume II.

Also important in later chapters is the question of how workers respond to changes in what we can call the "net real wage rate." This is the inflation-adjusted wage that the worker receives after accounting for any reduction in his inflation-adjusted real wage that results from his incurring an additional tax liability or from his sacrificing a government benefit by earning another dollar of labor income.

Suppose that Adam's boss pays him a gross wage of $50 for an hour's work. (We will ignore how inflation affects Adam's real wage for the purpose of this example.) Suppose further that either (1) Adam has to pay 25% of his wage in income tax or (2) he has to forego 25% of his wage under a means-tested welfare program from which he receives benefits. In either event, his net wage is $37.50 (= 0.75 × $50). It is to changes in this net wage that Adam will respond in adjusting his work-leisure calculus.

An important question for purposes of considering the efficiency (or "classical") effects of policy changes is how workers respond to changes in their net wage. The more they respond, the greater the amount of labor that will be supplied to producers for any increase in the net wage brought about changes in tax rates or benefit formulas.

One measure of this responsiveness is the Frisch elasticity of labor supply. As described by economist Casey Mulligan, whose work we will examine closely in Volume II, the Frisch elasticity

> measures how people adjust their work behavior in response to a one-time, temporary change in after-tax compensation (whereas the substitution elasticity measures how people adjust their work behavior in response to a permanent change in after-tax compensation). The Frisch elasticity equals the sum of the substitution elasticity and a measure of people's willingness to trade off work and consumption over time.

Mulligan considers Frisch elasticities between 0.4 and 1.1 (Mulligan 2012). The authors of another study report that the Congressional Budget Office uses Frisch elasticities that range from 0.27 to 0.53, with a central estimate of 0.40 (Reichling and Whalen 2012, p. 3). These elasticities become important when considering how reductions in tax rates or social benefits affect labor supply.

CHAPTER 4

Saving

In Chapter 3 we saw that the return to saving r enters into the decision whether to consume or save. There we alluded to the fact that the effect on saving of a rise in the return to saving depends on the relative strength of the substitution and income effects at work.

The substitution effect results from the fact that, with a higher r, the individual finds that each dollar added to saving brings a higher return in the form of increased future consumption than it did before. If r rises from 5 to 6%, the individual gets $1.06 to apply to next year's consumption for every dollar saved, rather than $1.05. This operates to increase saving. A rise in r can be thought of a rise in the price of current consumption, as measured by the amount of future consumption foregone for each dollar allocated to current consumption.

The income effect results from the fact that an increase in r makes it possible to increase current consumption, and therefore reduce current saving, without reducing future consumption. Suppose that when $r = 5\%$ the individual saves $10,000. By saving $10,000 this year, he will have $10,500 more to spend next year. If r rises to 6%, he could *reduce* his saving to $9,906 (= $10,500/1.06) this year and still have $10,500 more to spend next year, given the rise in r. (For the time being, ignore the fact that this rise in r would reduce the present value of his income.) This creates an income effect equal to the difference between $10,000 and $9,906, which is the $94 by which he could reduce his current saving and increase his current consumption without suffering any loss in future consumption.

If, in this example, the rise in r induces the individual to increase current consumption and therefore decrease current saving, we say that the income effect more than offsets the substitution effect. If it induces him to decrease current consumption and therefore increase current saving, then the substitution effect more than offsets the income effect. If it induces him to keep his current consumption and saving constant, then the two effects exactly offset each other. Thus, under this last possibility and in the current example, the individual would have $10,600 to spend next year, which is exactly 1 percentage point more (the difference between 5 and 6%) than what was available to spend before the interest rate rose by 1 percentage point.

Alternative Views of Saving

A question of central importance to economic policy is whether a rise in the return to saving, as brought about by a reduction in the taxes on the return to saving, will cause saving to rise and by how much. The relative strength of the income and substitution effects is one factor to be considered while addressing this question.

There is another factor to be considered, which has to do with how saving responds to changes in income, given that there is no change in r. The long-run, classical view is that the individual simultaneously chooses his level of work effort and saving toward optimizing his lifetime utility. In this view, any unexpected change in current income manifests itself in a change in planned consumption over the individual's future. If the individual unexpectedly sees an increase in current income, he will allocate only a small portion of that increase to current consumption, saving the remaining portion to finance future consumption.

In the short run, however, when there is low-employment equilibrium, brought about by either excess aggregate supply or excess aggregate demand, things are different. Individuals cannot optimize their consumption–saving choices because they cannot optimize their work–leisure choices. In a Keynesian slump, employers will not use all the labor services workers want to provide. In a suppressed inflation slump, workers will not provide all the labor services employers want to hire. In both instances, workers' current income *and* current consumption are constrained by an imbalance between aggregate supply and demand. Government policies that are effective at correcting that imbalance will manifest themselves mainly in increases in current consumption.

This presents an empirical question: Do government correctives for a perceived imbalance between aggregate supply and aggregate demand result mainly in an increase in current consumption or saving? If they result in more consumption, then the diagnosis and the corrective can be deemed successful. If they result in more saving, then the diagnosis was wrong and the policy was wrongly applied. We consider some modern evidence bearing on this matter in Volume II.

Going Back to the Classical Model

Proceeding in the spirit of the classical model, there are two central questions: (1) How do changes in the return to saving r affect saving and (2) how much of an effect on current consumption (and therefore current saving) do changes in current income have? Let's address the first question first.

In Chapter 3, we assumed the existence of a saver named Adam. In the interest of gender equity and of adding some variety to the exposition, let's switch decision makers from Adam to Eve, and let's imagine that the young Eve, now out of the Garden of Eden, is about to begin a career over which she expects her income to follow a predictable pattern, rising from year to year until retirement.

Eve understands that each year, her saving or borrowing decision affects her future income and therefore her future consumption. She understands that her earning power will max out only as she approaches retirement and then, as we assume here, drop to zero. But she also realizes that she has the option, when she is young, of spending either less than she earns (in which case she saves) or more than she earns (in which case she borrows). If she wants to save for a comfortable retirement, she can save when she is young so that she can spend more later. On the other hand, if she is in a hurry to spend when she is young, she can borrow (to a degree at least) against her future income to finance current consumption. Later we will consider the possibility that she would want to borrow when young, save when middle age, and then dissave when old. But the general idea is that Eve is not constrained to spend only (or all) her current income.

The reality, of course, is that Eve's expectations about her future income can change moment to moment, as can the return to her saving r. In this chapter, we think of r as "the" interest rate, the rate at which Eve can alternately lend or borrow money. To simplify our thinking about Eve's thinking, we can imagine that every January 1, she reassesses her income prospects and makes a forecast of r for the purpose of planning her consumption and therefore her saving for the year to come and that she does this every year going forward all the way to the end of her planning horizon.

In performing this annual recalculation, Eve recognizes r as serving two roles: For one thing it measures the return to saving and, likewise, the cost of borrowing. For another, it serves as the discount rate for calculating the present value of her future income. The higher the r, the greater the return to saving, the greater the cost of borrowing, and the lower the present value of future income. If Eve wants to use $1,000 of her income next year to buy a TV now, she can borrow $952.38 (= $1,000/1.05) now to apply to that purchase if r equals 5%, but only $909.09 if r equals 10%.

We presented this present-value accounting in Chapter 3 in our discussion of Adam's choice calculus. But there we posited Adam as being a saver. A better theory would account for the possibility that he or Eve could switch from being a saver to a borrower or vice versa. So how will a change in r affect the decision to save or borrow?

The question of how changes in r affect Eve's lending or borrowing depends on how r enters into her consumption–saving decision. (Remember that lending is positive saving and borrowing is negative saving or *dissaving*.) We will shortly go into some detail figuring out how the rational Eve would decide between consumption and saving, given whatever r she faces in the market for loanable funds.

Now let's turn to a second question. Suppose Eve hits the lottery and brings home a check for a million dollars. (We will ignore taxes and the fact that the actual immediate payoff from a lottery is always much less than the advertised payoff). Unless Eve is foolish, she will not blow through the entire million dollars on the spot. Rather, she will spread out the benefits of her prize over her future, which will be very long if she is very young. She might even care about her future children and their future children. So the question is how much of her prize will Eve spend when she cashes the check. This is part of the general question whether a surge in current income will have much of an effect on current consumption.

Expanding the Saver's Time Horizon

Recall that in our two-period model, we calculate saving in period 1 as

$$sav_1 = lay_1 - c_1. \tag{4.1}$$

We now allow that Eve plans her consumption and saving over as long a period of time as she wishes to consider. We treat this period as beginning with year 1 and ending with year n. We allow that Eve can save or dissave (which is to say, borrow) as much as she wishes during any year $t = 1, 2,..., n - 1$, given that she will consume all she can in period n. We also allow that she receives a combination of labor and capital income over the course of her lifetime. So her total y_t in any period t is

$$y_t = lay_t + nw_t, \tag{4.2}$$

where nw_t is capital or asset income.

Now

$$sav_t = y_t - c_t, \text{ and} \tag{4.3}$$

$$s_t = \frac{y_t - c_t}{y_t}, \quad t = 1, 2 ... n - 1. \tag{4.4}$$

Note that Eve's saving rate can be positive, negative, or zero: positive if she consumes less than she earns in income, in which event she uses part of her income to augment her asset holdings, zero if she consumes all of her income, and negative if she supplements her consumption by drawing down her asset holdings.[1] This definition of the saving rate is useful because it corresponds to the common-sense idea that peoples' saving rate will be negative when they are young or old, and likely to spend more than they earn, and positive when they are middle-aged, and likely to spend less than they earn, to pay off debts incurred when young to acquire assets to spend down when old.

---

[1] This is not the same as the conventional definition, according to which the saving rate equals personal saving divided by disposable personal income. Here there are no taxes, so disposable income equals personal income.

Now let's construct a specific *utility function*, which shows how many utiles Eve gets from consumption in any one period. A utility function that macroeconomists frequently use for this purpose is as follows:

$$u_t = \frac{c_t^{1-z}}{1-z}. \tag{4.5}$$

While this specification may look complicated, the reason that it is so popular is similar to the reason (as we shall see) that the Cobb-Douglas specification of the production function is so popular, namely, that it is easy to work with. We will shortly see why this is true. For now, the only thing that's new is the parameter z. The name of the reciprocal of z, $\frac{1}{z}$, is the *intertemporal elasticity of substitution* (IES), which measures the sensitivity of Eve's consumption (and therefore saving) decisions to differences between the return to saving r and her rate of time preference ρ, as considered in Chapter 3.

We have already seen that when an individual maximizes utility, he (or in this instance, she) satisfies the following equation for a two-period model where t is period 1 and $t+1$ is period 2:

$$MRS_{c_t c_{t+1}} = (1+r), \tag{4.6}$$

the left-hand side of which can be expanded to read:

$$MRS_{c_t c_{t+1}} = \frac{MU_{c_t}}{MU_{c_{t+1}}}(1+\rho). \tag{4.7}$$

Generalizing the two-period model to n periods and substituting equation (4.6) into equation (4.7), Eve maximizes utility when

$$\frac{MU_{c_t}}{MU_{c_{t+1}}}(1+\rho) = 1+r \text{ for all } t = 1, 2, n-1. \tag{4.8}$$

Now let's use an example to flesh out equation (4.8). Suppose that Eve's planned consumption is $50,000 in period t and $55,000 in period $t+1$, and let z equal 0.5. A $1 change in her consumption in period t will cause her utility to change by

$$MU_{c_t} = \frac{\Delta u_t}{\Delta c_t} = \frac{50,000^{1-0.5}}{1-0.5} - \frac{50,000^{1-0.5}}{1-0.5}$$
$$= 447.2181 - 447.2136 = 0.0045. \qquad (4.9)$$

Correspondingly, a $1 change in her consumption in period $t + 1$ will cause her utility to change by

$$MU_{c_{t+1}} = \frac{\Delta u_{t+1}}{\Delta c_{t+1}} = \frac{55,001^{1-0.5}}{1-0.5} - \frac{55,000^{1-0.5}}{1-0.5}$$
$$= 469.0458 - 469.0416 = 0.0043. \qquad (4.10)$$

Finally, assume that Eve's rate of time preference p equals 5%, so that

$$(1+p) = 1.05. \qquad (4.11)$$

Plugging the information from equations (4.9), (4.10), and (4.11) into the left-hand side of equation (4.8), we get

$$\frac{MU_{c_t}}{MU_{c_{t+1}}}(1+p) = 1 + r = \frac{0.0045}{0.0043}(1+0.05) = 1.10 \text{ (after rounding). } (4.12)$$

Then also from equation (4.7),

$$MRS_{c_t c_{t+1}} = 1.10. \qquad (4.13)$$

Equations (4.9) and (4.10) tell us that an additional dollar of period t consumption adds as much to Eve's period t utility as an additional $1.0465 (= 0.0045/0.0043) of period $t + 1$ consumption adds to her period $t + 1$ utility. If Eve gives up $1.00 of consumption in period $t + 1$, she loses 0.0043 utiles in period $t + 1$, but if she adds $1.00 dollar to her consumption in period t, she gains 0.0045 utiles in period t. So she can give up as much as $1.0465 of her period $t + 1$ consumption while increasing her period t consumption by $1 and at the same time keep the sum of her utilities over the two periods constant. But because a period-t utile is worth 5% more than a period $t + 1$ utile, she is willing to give up $1.10 (= 1.0465 × 1.05) of period $t + 1$ consumption for another dollar of period t consumption. If r equals 10%, she satisfies the equilibrium condition of equation (4.6).

Maximizing Intertemporal Utility

Now we get to find out why the specification of Eve's utility function in equation (4.5) is so popular. It turns out that, after a lot of mathematics using equation (4.5), as shown in the Appendix to this chapter, we can transform equation (4.6) into the following equation:

$$\frac{\Delta c}{c} = (r - \rho)\frac{1}{z} \; .^2 \tag{4.14}$$

This tells us that when Eve is maximizing utility, the percentage change in her consumption from one period to the next equals the difference between r and ρ multiplied by $\frac{1}{z}$, which we previously identified as Eve's intertemporal elasticity of substitution (IES). We can simplify even more by rewriting equation (4.14) as

$$\%\Delta c = (r - \rho)\,\text{IES}. \tag{4.15}$$

We can also now see exactly what IES means. The IES is the number of percentage points by which the desired consumption in the next period will exceed consumption in the current period for every percentage point by which r exceeds ρ. (Or, if ρ exceeds r, the number of percentage points by which desired consumption in the next period will fall below consumption in the current period for every percentage point by which ρ exceeds r.)

Before thinking more about what this equation says, let's see if Eve maximizes her utility by increasing her consumption from \$50,000 to \$55,000 going from period t to period $t + 1$. Her planned percentage change in consumption ($\%\Delta c$) is 10% (= \$5,000/\$50,000). The question is whether this planned percentage change in consumption will maximize her utility. According to equation (4.15), it does if $(r - \rho)$IES also equals 10%. Well, let's see if it does: First, $(r - \rho)$ equals (10% − 5%) or 5%. Next, because z equals 0.5, $1/z$, which is the IES for Eve, equals 2. Thus, we have 0.05×2 or 10%. Eve does, in fact, maximize her utility!

---

[2] This relies on a couple of mathematical tricks whereby we can approximate $\ln(1 + r) - \ln(1 + \rho)$ as $(r - \rho)$ and $\ln c_t - \ln c_{t-1}$ as $\frac{\Delta c}{c}$.

The utility function specified in equation (4.5) thus turns out to have a convenient property, which lies in the fact that the coefficient $1/z$ measures the sensitivity of the individual's consumption plan to the difference between r and ρ, which is to say, to the difference between the return to saving and the individual's time preference.

As we know, r and ρ can change from moment to moment, but there is little sacrifice in generality if we continue to think of Eve as revising her plans for her economic future every January 1. The questions for this chapter are (1) what will be her year-1 consumption and saving and (2) how would a change in r or in her current and future income affect her year-1 consumption.

According to the usual view of Eve's saving decision, she would put aside some fraction s of her disposable income each year based on some combination of future needs (the wish to own her own home, the education of her kids, her retirement, etc.). This is all right as far as it goes, but the rational Eve understands that the money she has available to apply to her saving now will affect her consumption in every year of her life going forward (just as her income in every year of her life going forward affects her ability to consume and save). So the rational Eve needs to put together some information in order to decide how much to consume and save in every year of her life starting now and going forward. Specifically, she needs to know:

1. what interest rate r to use in figuring out the return to saving and in discounting future consumption and income,
2. how much she prefers current utility over future utility, that is, what value to attach to her ρ,
3. how sensitive her future consumption will be to the difference between r and ρ, that is, what value to attach to her IES, and
4. the number of years n over which she wants to plan her economic future.

Knowing this, she can figure out how much of her income to allocate to her current-year consumption and therefore her current-year saving. Once she knows that, she can apply equation (4.15) to figure out her second-year consumption, and then again to figure out her third-year consumption, and so forth. (Keep in mind that her second-year consumption will equal her first-year consumption times $(1 + \%\Delta c)$, where $\%\Delta c$ is determined once she knows what values to assign to r, ρ, and IES.).

Again, understand that economists don't require Eve consciously to make all these calculations. The computer she carries around in her brain can do all that without her explicitly thinking about it. Yet, as strange as this might seem to the noneconomist, everything here is based on common sense. One way or another, Eve's consumption in 2019 will bear some relationship to her consumption in 2018. The greater the reward to saving (r), the less impatient she is for current consumption (the lower her ρ), and the more she wants to substitute future for current consumption, given the difference between r and p, the more she will want her next-period consumption to exceed her current-period consumption. And then also, the more she will want to save in the current period.

Suppose the computer in Eve's head has already solved equation (4.15) on January 1, 2018, and then, seconds after midnight, she finds out that r has unexpectedly risen. Because this raises the return to saving and the cost of borrowing, Eve will want to rethink her spending plans for the year to come and for every year thereafter. Because her spending plans and her saving plans are just opposite sides of the same coin, she will likewise want to rethink her saving plans.

The same would happen if her rate of time preference ρ or her IES changed. Then once Eve has adjusted the left-hand side of equation (4.15) accordingly she will be back in utility-maximizing equilibrium. But Eve needs to figure out her year-1 consumption and saving before she can figure out how much more (or less) to spend on consumption in year 2. Equation (4.15) just tells us the percentage by which she will want to change her consumption going from the current period to the next. Let's identify the current period as year 1. Then Eve still needs to figure out how much to consume in year 1, after which she can plot her consumption plans all the way to retirement.

Last Step

To figure out Eve's year-1 consumption, we need to reintroduce an assumption from Chapter 3, whereby Eve will set the present value of her current and future consumption in year 1 equal to the present value of her current and future income. Let's write that condition as

$$PV_y = PV_c. \tag{4.16}$$

Given that assumption and equation (4.5), we can find a coefficient v, which when multiplied by the present value of Eve's income will tell us how much she wants to consume in year 1. Generally, Eve's period-1 consumption is

$$c_1 = vPV_y, \tag{4.17}$$

her period-1 saving is

$$sav_1 = y_1 - vPV_y, \tag{4.18}$$

and her saving rate is

$$s_1 = \frac{y_1 - vPV_y}{y_1}. \tag{4.19}$$

The Appendix to this chapter shows how to calculate v. In general:

1. When IES >1, v varies inversely with r and directly with ρ, and when IES <1, v varies directly with r and inversely with ρ.
2. v depends only on the size of ρ when IES = 1, in which event v varies directly with ρ.
3. When IES = 1, v approaches $\rho/(1 + \rho)$ in value as n approaches infinity.

Point 1 means that saving will be greater the higher the r and higher the IES. Point 2 means that changes in r will not affect the fraction of PV_y that is allocated to saving when IES =1. This goes to the relative strength of the income and substitution effects. The income and substitution effects must just offset each other when IES = 1. To see why, recall the example with which this chapter began. There we saw that a 1-percentage-point rise in r this year would bring about a 1% rise in the funds available for consumption next year without the need to increase saving. The same applies here, but more generally: If p is constant and IES = 1, the percentage change in consumption from one year to the next will rise for every percentage point increase in r but without an increase in saving.

The reader may well (and should) question the validity of equation (4.16), given that the present value of lifetime consumption for some people will far exceed the present value of their income. Those people include people who are lucky enough to be born rich and some others who sustain themselves from government transfer payments. Given that 72% of disposable personal income comes from wages, this, sadly perhaps, is not a widespread problem. And even trust-fund babies can come to see the value of work as they look to pass along their legacy to their progeny.

How Changes in r Affect Saving

Whether saving does or does not rise in year 1, given a rise in r, also depends on how a rise in r affects the present value of income. Remember that year-1 consumption equals v times the present value of income and that year-1 saving equals year-1 income minus year-1 consumption. Because a rise in r will reduce the present value of future income, a rise in r will for that reason alone reduce current consumption and therefore increase current saving.

To put some numbers to this analysis, suppose that IES = 1 and that we are back to a two-period world. Then we know that Eve's desired percentage change in consumption from period 1 to period 2 will rise by one percentage point for every percentage point that r rises, p remaining constant. Now let's make some more assumptions:

- $r = 5\%$
- $p = 2\%$
- $y_1 = \$60,000$, and
- $y_2 = \$42,000$.

From the Appendix we can use this information to find v, which turns out to be 50.495%. (The shorter the individual's time horizon, the larger v.) Table 4.1 shows the results for period-1 saving and for periods 1 and 2 consumption.

Now let the interest rate rise to 6% while all the other assumptions remain unchanged. Table 4.2 provides the results.

We see that saving rose, but not because v fell. Saving rose entirely because the present value of income fell. When IES = 1, a rise in the interest rate therefore does not affect current consumption or current saving, except insofar as it reduces the present value of income.

A rise in r will induce Eve to increase her saving rate because it will reduce PV_y and therefore current consumption. Conversely, a fall in r will induce Eve to decrease her saving rate because it will increase PV_y and therefore current consumption. It is just that her saving rate will change more, the larger her IES.

Table 4.1 Two-period model (r = 5%)

PV_y	$100,000 [a]
c_1	$50,495 [b]
sav_1	$9,505 [c]
s_1	15.84% [d]
$sav_1(1 + r)$	9,980 [e]
c_2	$51,980 [f]
$\Delta c/c$	2.94% [g]

a = $60,000 + $42,000/(1.05); b = 0.50495 × $100,000; c = $60,000 − $50,495; d = $9,505/$60,000; e = $9,505 × (1 + 0.05); f = $42,000 + $9,980; g = ($51,980 − $50,495)/$50,495

Table 4.2 Two-period model (r = 6%)

PV_y	$99,623 [a]
c_1	$50,305 [b]
sav_1	$9,695 [c]
s_1	16.2% [d]
$sav_1(1 + r)$	10,277 [e]
c_2	$52,277 [f]
$\Delta c/c$	3.92% [g]

a = $60,000 + $42,000/(1.06); b = 0.50495 × $99,263; c = $60,000 − $50,305; d = $9,695/$60,000; e = $9,695 × (1 + 0.06); f = $42,000 + $10,277; g = ($52,277 − $50,305)/$50,305

Suppose that IES equals 1.5. Eve will want the percentage change in her consumption to equal 1.5 percentage points for every percentage point rise in r (again, holding ρ constant). The substitution effect of the rise in r will more than offset the income effect.

Let's make our analysis more realistic now by assuming that Eve takes her first job on her 22nd birthday and that the job offers a starting salary of $50,000. Eve expects to retire in 40 years, when she is 62, and expects to get a 5% raise each year she is on the job (which means she'll make about $335,000 dollars the last year she works!). We assume that, for convenience, the interest rate is initially also 5%. Finally, we assume that Eve has a rate of time preference of 2% and an IES of 1.5.

Discounted over Eve's 40-year working life, the present value of her income is $2,000,000. Given our assumptions, Eve's v is 2.77%, and her first-year consumption is $55,400 (see footnote a to Table 4.3). She plans that, during the first year of her career, her saving will be a negative $5,400 and her saving rate will therefore be –10.8%. Her planned year-2 consumption is $57,893, which, given the values assigned to r, ρ, and IES must be 4.5% greater than her year-1 consumption.

Now suppose that, just after Eve had planned out her current and future consumption, the interest rate rose unexpectedly to 6%. Eve's income stream remains unchanged, but her v falls to 2.53%.

The present value of her income stream falls to $1,672,452. Thus, she revises her plans so that she will consume $42,313 in the first year and $44,852 in the second. She will increase her first-year saving from –$5,400 to $7,687 and her saving rate from –10.8 to 15.4%.

We can infer that a given rise in the return to saving produces a larger rise in Eve's saving rate as her IES exceeds 1. But whatever the value of

Table 4.3 Lifetime model: Effects of a rise in r

	r	v	PV1	c_1	c_2	sav_1	s_1
Initial values	5%	2.77%	$2,000,000	$55,400[a]	$57,893[b]	–$5,400[c]	–10.8%[d]
Values after r rises	6%	2.53%	$1,672,452	$42,313[e]	$44,852[f]	$7,687[g]	15.4%[h]

a = 0.0277 × $2,000,000; b = $55,400 × (1 + ((5% – 2%) × 1.5)); c = $50,000 – $55,400; d = –$5,400/$50,000; e = 0.0253 × $1,672,452; f = $42,313 × (1 + ((6% – 2%) × 1.5)); g = $50,000 – $42,313; h = $7,687/$50,000

Table 4.4 Effects of IES on the saving rate

IES	v	s_1
0.1	5.34%	–113%
0.5	4.52%	–81%
1.0	3.58%	–43%
2.0	2.08%	17%
2.5	1.52%	39%

her IES, v will always be small when the planning period extends well out to the future. To see this, let's consider a few more examples. In Table 4.4 we assume that $\rho = 0.02$, $n = 40$, $r = 0.05$, and $lay_1 = \$50,000$. The larger Eve's IES, the smaller her v and the larger her s.

Assume again that Eve's first-year income is $50,000 and that she has a $v = 2.77\%$. Now she hits the lottery and brings home $1,000,000. Eve's PV_y rises from $2,000,000 to $3,000,000. Given her v, her consumption will rise from $55,400 to $83,100. After winning $1,000,000 she will increase her current-year consumption by only $27,700! This dampens any hope of economic recovery through a fiscal stimulus, a matter to which we will return in Volume II.

As shown in the Appendix, these calculations are greatly simplified if we assume that IES = 1 and n is large. Then

$$v = \frac{\rho}{1 + \rho}. \qquad (4.20)$$

If, under these conditions, $\rho = 2\%$, a million-dollar bonus in year 1 will increase consumption in that year, and in every year to follow, by $19,608.

The Permanent Income Hypothesis

These observations are consistent with the *permanent income hypothesis,* which states that people make spending decisions according to how a change in current-period income affects their permanent income. We see that if the rational Eve experiences a change in her current income (even a change of $1 million) she will adjust her current consumption according to how that change affects the present value of her current and future income and according to the size of v. And if Eve has a long planning horizon even large changes in her current income will have small effects on this PV_y. So what is her "permanent income?"

One idea that motivates the concept of permanent income is that people will want to smooth out their consumption stream over their lifetimes to whatever degree is possible. The foregoing discussion provides examples in which the individual will have a consumption schedule that slopes steeply upward or steeply downward over her lifetime, depending on the size of r, ρ, and the IES. A high r and a low ρ indicate high saving at the beginning of the planning period but high consumption at the end. Just the opposite is true for a low r and a high ρ.

This means that actual income will vary from year to year, depending on a great many factors (including such things as lottery winnings), while consumption will follow some more or less steady path, depending on how the individual wants to structure his or her consumption over the planning period. Think of permanent income, then, as the individual's consumption stream, however arranged, over his future. Hitting the lottery will always have a much smaller effect on permanent income than on current income since the lucky winner will want to spread his winnings out more or less evenly over her future.

There is an argument to the effect that permanent income, so defined, will be flat over that future even as actual current income rises and falls. Let's see why the individual would not want to have a steeply rising or steeply falling consumption curve over her future.

If Eve is a high saver at the beginning of her life, her consumption will steadily rise over the course of her lifetime and the marginal utility of consumption will steadily decline. Using the notation developed earlier, MU_{c_t} would be high relative to $MU_{c_{t+1}}$. It seems that she would want to move some of her consumption from her later years, when the utility she would lose by taking a dollar out of consumption is low, relative to her early years, when the utility she would gain by adding a dollar to consumption is high. If she were to do this, MU_{c_t} would fall and $MU_{c_{t+1}}$ would rise until, in the limit, they were equal. But then, as we see from equation (4.8), ρ would then have to rise until it was equal to r.

Conversely, if Eve is a high borrower at the beginning of her life, her consumption will steadily fall over the course of her lifetime and the marginal utility of consumption will steadily rise. MU_{c_t} would be low relative to $MU_{c_{t+1}}$. It seems that she would want to move some of her consumption from her early years, when the utility she would lose by taking a dollar out of consumption is low, to her later years, when the utility she would gain by adding a dollar to consumption is high. If she were to do this, MU_{c_t} would rise and $MU_{c_{t+1}}$ would fall until, in the limit, they were equal. This time p would have to fall until it was equal to r.

This logic argues for a saving strategy that brings the rate of time preference p into line with the interest rate r. Return to equation (4.15) and consider what it means if $p = r$. Mathematically, the individual sets $\%\Delta c$ equal to zero for all periods going forward and thus equalizes consumption from one year to the next over the entire planning period. What seems intuitively plausible is that Eve would want to even out her consumption over life as much as practical. Every entrant into the labor force can reasonably expect his or her earnings to be low at first, then rise, and then drop precipitously upon retirement.

Neither Adam nor Eve will, however, want to eat sardines when young and old but then gorge on filet mignon when middle aged. In the language of economics, the marginal utility of the individual's income will be high when his earnings are low, that is when he is young and when he is old, and the marginal utility of his income will be low when his earnings are high, that is when he is middle aged. Insofar as he wants to equalize the marginal utility of consumption across his lifetime, he will dissave (borrow) when young, save when middle aged, and dissave (use up assets) when old. Operationally, in our planning model, this means adjusting p to be equal to r, so that consumption is equal across the individual's planning period.

This in turn means that in order for aggregate saving to be positive, we need to have a lot of middle-aged income earners who are accumulating assets even as younger and retired individuals dissave. It also means that we need tax policies that encourage saving, a matter taken up in Chapter 7.

Figure 4.1 illustrates the results of this strategy for the example provided in the first row of Table 4.3, with the difference that p and r are both assumed to equal 5%. There Eve's annual income rises from \$50,000 in year 1 to \$335,000 in year 40, after which it drops to zero. (We assume that Eve spends her golden years living with her children, who generously

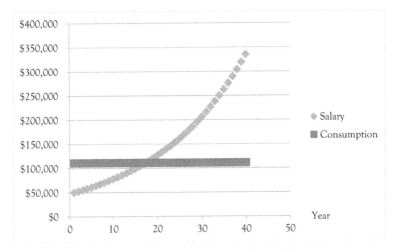

Figure 4.1 Illustration of permanent income hypothesis

subsidize her consumption beyond her planning period to her death.) She fixes her annual consumption at $111,000 per year from year 1 to year 40.

Thus $111,000 per year is Eve's *permanent income*. It is the consumption she would enjoy if she equalized her consumption over her lifetime, given her earnings expectations and the value of *r*. Eve's permanent income is to be distinguished from her temporary income. If at some point in her life Eve wins $10,000 in the lottery, her temporary income will rise by $10,000, but her permanent income will hardly rise at all.

Eve would face myriad practical obstacles to a strategy that had her spending twice as much as she earns in her early years. There are practical obstacles to any consumption plan that requires borrowing against future income. In practice, young people dissave by taking out student loans, borrowing from relatives, and cashing in any inheritances they are lucky enough to receive. But a confident young Eve cannot go to her bank and take out a loan to buy a luxurious house, on the promise that she can pay off the loan without any problem in a decade or so. *Liquidity constraints* limit the practicality of any scheme requiring substantial borrowing against future earnings.

Yet the example is based on common sense and yields a handy tool for estimating the effect of an increase in current income on current consumption. As shown in the Appendix, *v* reduces to

$$v = \frac{r}{1+r} \qquad (4.21)$$

if we assume that $\rho = r$ and that n is large. Thus, if r equals 5% and if Eve wins $1,000,000 in the lottery, her spending in year 1 and in every year thereafter will rise by $47,619. This can be considered to be the classical analog of the *marginal propensity to consume* of the Keynesian model.

There is one overriding conclusion about the effects of windfall gains that can be taken from this chapter, which is that any such gain will yield a small increase in current consumption because of the desirability of "consumption smoothing," which means spreading the benefits over the future rather than just taking them all at once. This bodes ill for government policies aimed at stimulating current consumption through tax rebates and the like.

In the aggregate, saving is positive. But if aggregate saving is positive year after year going forward then individual savers are regularly, and on balance, taking part of their income and putting it into income-earning assets on which they plan to draw in future years to finance their planned consumption. The existence of a positive national saving rate depends on the preponderance in the labor force of individuals who anticipate income decreases as they age and who want to accumulate income-earning assets during their peak earning years in order to pay off loans taken when young and to save for retirement.

Policy Implications

We shall see in Chapter 6 that a government policy that succeeds in raising the saving rate s can bring about an increase in real GDP per person. In Chapter 7, we will see how government can increase the rate of return to saving r and thus increase the individual's saving rate by reducing taxes on capital income. The ability of government to increase s by increasing r depends, as we have seen, on the size of the IES. The greater the IES, the more effective are government policies aimed at increasing s. But is the IES large enough for those policies to be effective?

Economist Robert Hall has offered what is probably the most pessimistic assessment of the prospects for increasing the saving rate through the removal of tax deterrents to saving. As he puts it, his analyses provide "little basis for a conclusion that the behavior of aggregate consumption in the United States in the 20th century reveals an important positive value of the intertemporal elasticity of substitution" (Hall 1988, p. 356). See also (Braun and Jakajima 2012). Hall finds that increases in r have almost no effect (and might have a negative effect) on saving.

In contrast, Jonathan Gruber finds that the "estimated EIS [elasticity of intertemporal substitution, same as the IES] is very large, larger than most estimates from the previous literature, and this estimate is robust to a wide variety of specification checks" (Gruber 2013, p. 4). Gruber finds the value to be around 2 (Gruber 2013, p. 24). In his book *The Redistribution Recession,* Casey Mulligan puts the IES at 1.35 (Mulligan 2012, p. 152).

Perhaps, on the other hand, the size of the IES becomes less important when we consider the implications of the assumption, maintained throughout this chapter, that people base their current saving decisions on planned lifetime consumption. In this regard, David Romer considers the scenario in which "r is slightly larger than ρ and that the elasticity of substitution is small." These assumptions "imply that consumption rises slowly over the individual's lifetime. But with a long lifetime, this means that consumption is much larger at the end of the life than the beginning." Then, given that income is constant,

> this in turn implies that the individual gradually builds up considerable savings over the first part of his or her life and gradually decumulates them over the remainder. As a result, when horizons are finite but long, wealth holdings may be highly responsive to the interest rate in the long run even if the intertemporal elasticity of substitution is small (Romer 2012, pp. 383–84).

This chapter delved into the saving calculus of the individual. In the next chapter we consider how saving decisions match up with capital investment decisions to determine investment and the equilibrium capital stock.

Appendix A

First we set the present value of utility equal to the individual's consumption stream discounted by ρ:

$$PVu = \frac{c_1^{1-z}}{1-z} + \frac{1}{1+\rho}\frac{c_2^{1-z}}{1-z} + \frac{1}{(1+\rho)^2}\frac{c_3^{1-z}}{1-z} + \dots + \frac{1}{(1+\rho)^{n-1}}\frac{c_n^{1-z}}{1-z} \quad (4A.1)$$

Next we write out the formula for the present value of consumption:

$$PV_c = c_1 + \frac{c_2}{1+r} + \frac{c_3}{(1+r)^2} + \dots + \frac{c_n}{(1+r)^{n-1}}. \quad (4A.2)$$

We can write the individual's utility maximization problem in terms of the Lagrangian expression:

$$Z = PV_u + \lambda \left(PVc - \left(c_1 + \frac{c_2}{1+r} + \frac{c_3}{(1+r)^2} + \dots + \frac{c_n}{(1+r)^{n-1}} \right) \right). \quad (4A.3)$$

Maximizing (4A.3) we get

$$\frac{\partial Z}{\partial c_t} = \frac{c_t^{-z}}{(1+\rho)^{t-1}} - \lambda \frac{1}{(1+r)^{t-1}} = 0, \quad (4A.4)$$

for all $t = 2,\dots, n$.
and

$$\frac{c_t^{-z}}{c_{t+1}^{-z}} = \frac{1+r}{1+\rho}, \quad (4A.5)$$

where

$$c_t^{-z} = MU_{c_t} \text{ and} \quad (4A.6)$$

$$c_{t+1}^{-z} = MU_{c_{t+1}}. \quad (4A.7)$$

Then

$$\frac{c_{t+1}}{c_t} = \left(\frac{1+r}{1+\rho} \right)^{1/z} \text{ and} \quad (4A.8)$$

$$c_{t+1} = \left(\frac{1+r}{1+\rho}\right)^{1/z} c_t,$$ (4A.9)

for all $t = 1,\ldots, n$.

We can further simplify this by taking logarithms of both sides of (4A.8):

$$\ln c_{t+1} - \ln c_t = \frac{1}{z}\left[\ln(1+r) - \ln((1+\rho)\right], \text{ to get}$$ (4A.10)

$$\frac{\Delta c}{c} = (r - p)\frac{1}{z}.$$ (4A.11)

Now we set the present value of consumption equal to the present value of income:

$$PV_y = y_1 + \frac{y_2}{1+r} + \frac{y_3}{(1+r)^2} + \ldots + \frac{y_n}{(1+r)^{n-1}} = PVc.$$ (4A.12)

Letting

$$q = \left(\frac{1+r}{1+\rho}\right)^{1/z},$$ (4A.13)

we can write:

$$PV_y = c_1\left[1 + \frac{q}{1+r} + \left(\frac{q}{(1+r)}\right)^2 + \left(\frac{q}{(1+r)}\right)^3 + \ldots + \left(\frac{q}{(1+r)}\right)^{n-1}\right].$$ (4A.14)

Then we can solve for c_1 by multiplying both sides of (4A.14) by $\frac{q}{1+r}$ and subtracting, to get

$$\frac{q}{1+r}PV_y = c_1\left[\frac{q}{1+r} + \left(\frac{q}{(1+r)}\right)^2 + \left(\frac{q}{(1+r)}\right)^3 + \ldots + \left(\frac{q}{(1+r)}\right)^n\right].$$ (4A.15)

Solving,

$$PV_y\left(1 - \frac{q}{1+r}\right) = c_1\left[1 - \left(\frac{q}{(1+r)}\right)^n\right], \text{ and}$$ (4A.16)

$$c_1 = \frac{1 - \dfrac{q}{1+r}}{1 - \left(\dfrac{q}{(1+r)}\right)^n} PV_y. \tag{4A.17}$$

If we let

$$v = \frac{1 - \dfrac{q}{1+r}}{1 - \left(\dfrac{q}{(1+r)}\right)^n}, \tag{4A.18}$$

then

$$c_1 = vPV_y.$$

Note that if the intertemporal elasticity of substitution, $\dfrac{1}{z}$, equals 1, q becomes $\left(\dfrac{1+r}{1+\rho}\right)$ and

$$c_1 = \frac{1 - \dfrac{1+r}{1+\rho}\dfrac{1}{1+r}}{1 - \left(\dfrac{1+r}{1+\rho}\dfrac{1}{1+r}\right)^n} PV_y = \frac{\dfrac{\rho}{1+\rho}}{1 - \left(\dfrac{1}{1+\rho}\right)^n}. \tag{4A.19}$$

Then, as n approaches infinity, (4A.19) becomes

$$c_1 = \frac{\rho}{1+\rho} PV_y, \tag{4A.20}$$

so that

$$v = \frac{\rho}{1+\rho}. \tag{4A.21}$$

We can also see that if $r = \rho$, then

$$v = \frac{\dfrac{r}{1+r}}{1 - \left(\dfrac{1}{(1+r)}\right)^n}. \tag{4A.22}$$

Finally, in that case, as n approaches infinity,

$$v = \frac{r}{1+r}.$$

(4A.23)

CHAPTER 5

Capital and Labor

An important issue that arises in macroeconomics has to do with how the economy performs, given that it is in a classical state of full employment. Recall Alan Blinder's comment, noted in Chapter 1, about utilizing "inputs more efficiently." This is called the efficiency or allocative problem in economics and is a problem that economic agents solve in the classical model. The efficiency problem can be seen as one aspect of the overall coordination problem.

In this chapter, we will see how individual economic agents solve this problem as it relates to capital and labor. In the preceding chapter, we considered in detail how economic agents solve the problem of how much to save and therefore how much financial capital to provide to the users of financial capital, that is, investors. Here we will combine that decision with the choice calculus of producers as it relates to the use of financial capital and thereby the acquisition of physical capital.

Decisions to Save and Invest

In previous chapters, we used the letter r to indicate the rate of interest. What we didn't do is include any discussion of inflation and how that might affect r, given that r represents the inflation-adjusted, *real interest rate*.

If someone buys an IOU for $100 and if the inflation rate is zero, he will have received a real rate of return of 5% if he can sell or redeem that IOU for $105 a year later. More specifically, if a slice of pizza costs $1.00, he will surrender purchasing power over 100 slices when he buys the IOU and will be able to buy 105 slices when he sells or redeems it.

Suppose, however, that prices rise by 1% over the course of the loan, so that the price of a slice of pizza rises to $1.01. Then the $105 dollars will permit him to buy only $103.96 worth of pizza, or at the new, inflated price, 103.96 slices. His real return on the loan will be only

3.96%. It turns out that the willingness to lend money (and more generally to provide financial capital) depends on his expectation of inflation.

In order to flesh out this point, let's go to a post-Garden-of-Eden world where Adam wants to borrow $10,000 from Eve for the purpose of buying a pizza oven for Adam's Pizzeria. We say that Adam wants to sell Eve an IOU or a bond for $10,000. We designate the nominal interest rate that Eve will demand as R.

Adam expects his investment in the oven to yield a certain amount of income per dollar invested. This is the marginal product of capital, which we designate MP_k. Adam also expects the oven to undergo economic depreciation annually at the rate of d. The cost to him of buying the oven in year 1 is $P_1 \Delta k$, where P_1 is an index of year-1 prices and Δk is the cost of the oven, which in this case is $10,000. By setting $P_1 = 1$, we set $P_1 \Delta k = \$10,000$.

We can make the underlying concepts more concrete by introducing some more numbers. Thus, suppose that the MP_k equals 7%, so that every dollar sunk into the purchase of an oven yields 7 cents in new revenue. Also let the economic depreciation rate, d, equal 1%, so that the oven annually loses 1% of its value through wear and tear. If prices rise by, say, 4.0% over the course of the year, the resale value of the oven will rise to $P_2 \Delta K = \$10,400$, ignoring depreciation. The oven will, however, have depreciated by 1%, leaving him with an oven worth $10,296, which is $296 more than he paid for the oven. By the first of the following year, Adam will have added $728.00 ($= P_2 \Delta k MP_k$) to his sales for having bought the oven. This adds up to a payout of $1,024 ($= \$296 + \$728$) on a purchase of $10,000 and a return of 10.24% ($= \$1,024/\$10,000$). We can use this information to provide a formula for the nominal rate of return on Adam's investment:

$$NRR = \frac{P_2(1 + MP_k - d)\Delta k - P_1 \Delta k}{P_1 \Delta k}, \tag{5.1}$$

Letting $\hat{P}$ equal the rate of inflation,

$$P_2 = P_1(1 + \hat{P}). \tag{5.2}$$

Equation (5.1) then becomes

$$NRR = \frac{P_1(1+\widehat{P})(1+MP_k-d)\Delta k - P_1\Delta k}{P_1\Delta k}, \qquad (5.3)$$

or here

$$NRR = \frac{1.04(1+0.07-0.01)\$10,000-1(\$10,000)}{1(\$10,000)}$$
$$= \frac{\$11,024-\$10,000}{\$10,000} = 10.24\%. \qquad (5.4)$$

Equation (5.1) simplifies to

$$NRR = (1-\widehat{P})(1+MP_k-d)-1, \qquad (5.5)$$

which simplifies still further to

$$NRR \approx MP_k - d + \widehat{P} = 0.07 - 0.01 + 0.04 = 10\%. \qquad (5.6)$$

Next let's distinguish between Adam's actual rate of return, calculated in equation (5.4), from his expected rate of return. This will depend in part on what he expects the inflation rate to be. Given that he expects the inflation rate to be $\widehat{P}_A^E$, he will expect the period-2 price level to be

$$P_{A2}^E = P_1\left(1+\widehat{P}_A^E\right). \qquad (5.7)$$

His expected nominal return is then written as

$$NRR^E = \frac{P_1\left(1+\widehat{P}_A^E\right)(1+MP_k-d)\Delta k - P_1\Delta k}{P_1\Delta k} \qquad (5.8)$$

or

$$NRR^E = \left(1+\widehat{P}_A^E\right)(1+MP_k-d)-1, \qquad (5.9)$$

which simplifies still further to

$$NRR^E \approx MP_k - d + \widehat{P}_A^E. \qquad (5.10)$$

We can see from equations (5.5) and (5.9) that his expected and actual nominal return are both 10.24% if actual inflation $\widehat{P}$ equals Adam's expected inflation $\widehat{P}_A^E$. In reality, the two numbers will seldom be exactly equal, though we will consider in what follows how they would *tend* to be equal. Suppose they are not equal. Suppose that $\widehat{P}_A^E = 3.0\%$ while $\widehat{P} = 4.0\%$ as before. Then

$$NRR^E = (1+0.03)(1+0.07-0.01)-1 = 9.18\%, \qquad (5.11)$$

and

$$NRR = (1+0.04)(1+0.07-0.01)-1 = 10.24\%. \qquad (5.12)$$

We see that there are two measures of the return to investment: There is the expected or (as it is sometimes called) the *ex ante* return, and there is the actual or *ex post* return. The difference arises from elements in the equation for the nominal return for which the investor does not have perfect foresight. Here we focus on inflation. (The investor might equally lack perfect foresight in estimating the marginal product of capital and the depreciation rate.) In this example, Adam will want to borrow the money needed to finance his investment if Eve is willing to lend it to him at an interest rate not greater than 9.18%. If the actual return turns out to be 10.24%, so much the better for Adam and so much the worse for Eve, in that she underestimated the inflation rate and therefore overestimated the return on her loan in charging Adam 9.18% for the loan.

So now let's see whether Eve will want to lend Adam the $10,000 he needs for his investment, which is to say whether she will want to buy the IOU Adam wants to sell her. Adam will be willing to sell the IOU as long as she doesn't demand interest exceeding 9.18% on the loan.

Eve, for her part, has in mind some return on the loan that she expects to receive. She knows that her real return, r, will be lower than her nominal return R, which is the interest rate she will charge Adam, if prices rise over the course of the loan. Suppose she wants to get real return r^E of 6.0%, and suppose she expects inflation to run at 2.0% over the period of the loan, which we set at one year. At what value should she set R?

Let's attack the problem by writing an equation for what the real value of her bond (which can be an IOU bought from Adam) will be when it matures.

$$b_2 = \frac{b_1}{P_2}(1 + R),$$ (5.13)

where b_1 is the amount that she pays for the bond, and b_2 is the real value of the bond a year after she buys it. If Eve lends \$10,000 to Adam, so that b_1 = \$10,000, if she lends that money at a rate of 5%, as specified by the bond, and if the inflation rate is 2%, then that bond will be worth \$10,294 in real dollars when it matures a year later.

Now if we designate Eve's expected inflation rate to be $\hat{P}_E^E$, we can rewrite (5.13) as

$$b_2 = \frac{b_1}{P_1}\frac{(1 + R)}{(1 + \hat{P}_E^E)} = \frac{b_1}{P_1}(1 + r^E), \text{ so that}$$ (5.14)

$$(1 + r^E) = \frac{1 + R}{1 + \hat{P}_E^E},$$ (5.15)

where r^E is the real return on the bond that Eve wants to receive.

We can calculate r^E as

$$r^E = \frac{1 + R}{1 + \hat{P}_E^E} - 1,$$ (5.16)

or, more simply,

$$r^E \approx R - \hat{P}_E^E.$$ (5.17)

We can then use equation (5.15) to solve for the nominal rate of return on the loan that she must demand, given $\hat{P}_E^E$ and given that she wants to receive a real return of r^E.

$$R = (1 + r^E)(1 + \hat{P}_E^E) - 1.$$ (5.18)

Or, if r^E = 6%, and if Eve's expected inflation rate is 2%, then

$$R = (1 + 0.06)(1 + 0.02) - 1 = 8.12\%.$$ (5.19)

With a little algebra and simplification, we get

$$R \approx r^E + \widehat{P}_E^E = 0.06 + 0.02 = 8\%. \tag{5.20}$$

If NRR^E in equation (5.10) comes to 9%, Adam and Eve will find it mutually beneficial for Eve to lend to Adam.

Because Eve cannot predict inflation with perfect accuracy, however, we have to allow that the actual real return on the loan may be different from her intended real return.

With that in mind, her actual real return on the loan becomes

$$r = \frac{1+R}{1+\widehat{P}} - 1 \tag{5.21}$$

or

$$r \approx R - \widehat{P}, \tag{5.22}$$

where $\widehat{P}$ is the actual rate of inflation. If $\widehat{P}$ turns out to exceed $\widehat{P}_E^E$, Eve will be disappointed to learn that her actual return was less than her intended return.

We can figure that as long as NRR^E exceeds R, Adam will be willing to borrow from Eve and that as long as R permits Eve to enjoy her expected return r^E, she will be willing to lend to Adam. However, the gap between NRR^E and R will shrink as Adam borrows more from Eve, owing to the *law of diminishing returns*, which will manifest itself in a decline in MP_k and owing to Eve desiring a greater real return as she lends more.

We will spell out that process in greater detail in the following paragraphs. For now, let's observe that Adam and Eve reach an equilibrium in their transactions when Adam's NRR^E equals Eve's R, so that

$$\left(1 + \widehat{P}_A^E\right)\left(1 + MP_k - d\right) - 1 = \left(1 + \widehat{P}_E^E\right)\left(1 + r^E\right) - 1. \tag{5.23}$$

That is, Adam will continue borrowing from Eve and Eve will continue lending to Adam until his expected nominal return equals hers.

At this point we make a bold assumption, which is that in the long run everyone has the same expectation of inflation. Wrong as this must be in practice, it has an intuitively plausible foundation, based on the idea of *rational expectations* in economics. Because everyone on both sides of the capital market must make some assessment of future prices in making a decision whether to provide or use financial capital, each actor will use the best information available. As discussed in Volume II, Chapter 1, one model of expected inflation is that inflation equals the growth of the money supply. Thus all that Adam and Eve, right along with Cain and Abel, have to do is watch the growth of the money supply, information on which is available to all, in order to form a rational expectation of $\hat{P}$. Thus we now have a state of affairs in which $\hat{P}_A^E = \hat{P}_E^E = \hat{P}$ so that

$$(1 + \hat{P})(1 + MP_k - d) - 1 = (1 + \hat{P})(1 + r) - 1. \qquad (5.24)$$

Note the assumptions we have to make in order to get this equation. We must assume that Adam and Eve not only have the same expectations of inflation but also that their expectations are accurate and that they have reached equilibrium in their transactions with each other. This is what rational expectations is all about. Proponents of this point of view will argue that if anyone's foresight is wrong, he will learn from his mistakes and arrive at expectations that are in line with reality.

What we lose here in plausibility, at any rate, we gain in simplification. That's because equation (5.24) reduces to

$$MP_k = r + d. \qquad (5.25)$$

How do Adam and Eve reach this equilibrium? Going back to our example involving Adam and his pizza oven, suppose each dollar he spends on an oven yields $.08 in revenue (in "real" dollars). Then

$$MP_k = 8\%. \qquad (5.26)$$

Now what does it cost Adam to get his oven? What is his *cost of capital?* Well, suppose Eve demands a real return of 6% on her loan and that the depreciation rate for the oven is 1%. In that event his cost of capital, *cc*, is

$$r^E + d = 0.07 \qquad (5.27)$$

Because $MP_k > cc$, Adam will want to acquire the financing to expand his stock of ovens. If it had turned out that $MP_k < cc$, then the last dollar he spent on ovens would have cost more than it yielded in new revenue, and he would have wanted to sell at least some of his oven capital to a different pizza maker. In general, Adam will want to expand his capital stock as long as $MP_k > cc$ and contract it as long as $MP_k < cc$.

Now what about Eve?

In Chapter 3, we imagined that the individual adjusted his consumption–saving decision to a given real interest rate r. The individual adjusts his current-period consumption to the point where his $MRS_{c_t c_{t+1}} = 1 + r$.

In that chapter, we treated the interest rate as a datum, determined by the market. Here we treat it as a magnitude to be determined through interaction of borrower and lender. As long as Eve, the lender, demands only a small amount of future consumption in order to provide another dollar of financing, that is, as long as her $MRS_{c_t c_{t+1}}$ is low, she will expect only a low return r^E on a dollar lent to Adam. On the other hand, if her $MRS_{c_t c_{t+1}}$ is high, she will expect a high return.

Now think of what this means to the return to Adam on his acquisition of ovens, as opposed to his cost of acquiring them. If Adam has borrowed very little from Eve and if his stock of ovens is therefore low, his MP_k will be high relative to Eve's r^E. MP_k will exceed cc, and Adam will want to expand his oven stock.

On the other hand, if Adam has already borrowed a great deal from Eve, his MP_k will be low, owing to the law of diminishing returns. For her part, Eve's $MRS_{c_t c_{t+1}}$, and therefore her r^E will be high, owing to the law of the diminishing marginal rate of substitution of c_t for c_{t+1}. (If her $MRS_{c_t c_{t+1}}$ falls when she expands c_t, it will rise when she contracts it by lending to Adam.) Adam's cc will exceed his MP_k, and he will want to sell off some of his oven stock. Then in equilibrium, after these adjustments and given that $r^E = r$,

$$cc = r + d. \qquad (5.28)$$

In this state, also, the equilibrium condition

$$MRS_{c_t c_{t+1}} = 1 + r \qquad (5.29)$$

will be satisfied, as will equation (5.24).

We can think of Adam as wanting to expand his holdings of capital just to the point where the marginal product of capital equals the cost to him of obtaining that capital. We write this condition as

$$MP_k = cc, \tag{5.30}$$

so that his preferences line up with Eve's:

$$MP_k = MRS_{c_t c_{t+1}} - 1 + d. \tag{5.31}$$

From Chapter 2, equation (2.26) we get:

$$I + NX = S + (T - G). \tag{5.32}$$

If NX and $T - G$ are both zero, we see that every dollar of capital spending (as on pizza ovens) requires a dollar of private saving. From the foregoing analysis, the cost-of-capital (cc) curve for the entire economy will be upward sloping, owing to the law of the diminishing marginal rate of substitution of c_t for c_{t+1}. The MP_k curve, on the other hand, will be downward sloping owing to the law of diminishing returns. We can therefore portray market equilibrium as in Figure 5.1, where cc^* is the equilibrium cost of capital and K^* the equilibrium capital stock.

Let's consider some features of this equilibrium. Let the equilibrium stock of ovens, expressed in Figure 5.1, be $1 million. Now suppose that

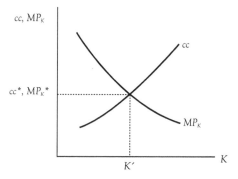

Figure 5.1 The supply and demand for capital

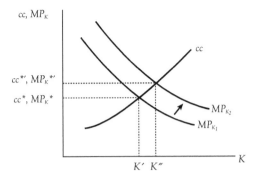

Figure 5.2 **An increase in the demand for capital**

technological progress or some other factor causes MP_K to shift upward, as in Figure 5.2. Suppose further that at the new equilibrium, the capital stock equals $1.5 million. Net investment will come to $500,000. Given that $d = 1\%$, gross investment is

$$I = \Delta K + dK = \$500,000 + .01 \times \$1,000,000 = \$510,000, \qquad (5.33)$$

which must be matched by an equal amount of saving.

In a static equilibrium, K will reach a level $K^{*'}$ and r will rise to $r^{*'}$, at which point ΔK equals zero and saving equals depreciation dK. We will consider what a more realistic "dynamic" equilibrium looks like in the next chapter.

International Capital Movements

It is appropriate at this point to take into account the fact that capital flows across national borders in response to differences in interest rates, expectations of inflation, and exchange rate variations. Now, considering the multiplicity of countries involved, it is necessary to enter an even more rarefied atmosphere, in which there are only two countries. Let's call them the United States and Europe, which we label as ROW (for the rest of the world). Each country has its own currency, the dollar and the euro, and each country lets its currency fluctuate freely against the other. Borrowers and lenders can move financial capital and goods seamlessly across national borders.

The reader can probably see where this is headed, which is toward the conclusion that there will emerge a single, global real interest rate r. But rather than just give out the ending, let's see how we get there.

To get there, let's add another strong assumption, whereby it is just as easy for you or me to buy things in Boston as it is to buy them in, say, Paris. That assumption permits us to assume *purchasing power parity*, whereby exchange rates will adjust in such a way as to make every good as costly in "real" terms in one country as they are in another. In the context of the current example, there is some exchange rate ε, equal to the dollar price of a euro, that satisfies the equation

$$\varepsilon = \frac{P^{US}}{P^{ROW}} = 2, \tag{5.34}$$

where P^{US} is an index for the prices of goods in the United States and P^{ROW} an index for the prices of goods in Europe (i.e., the rest of the world). To give this further concreteness, let's return to our pizza-only world and assume that the dollar price of a slice of pizza is 1 and that the euro price of a slice of pizza is 0.5. Then the dollar price of a euro must be

$$\varepsilon = \frac{1.00}{0.50} = 2. \tag{5.35}$$

To see what is going on here, imagine that the Boston price of the pizza slice suddenly rose to $2.00. Then Bostonians would convert dollars into euros, buying 0.5 euros on the dollar, and use those euros to buy pizza in Paris, where a dollar's worth of euros buys them a whole slice of pizza, compared to the half of slice that a dollar now buys in Boston. This would increase the demand for euros and decrease the demand for dollars until the exchange rate depreciated to

$$\varepsilon = \frac{2.00}{0.50} = 4. \tag{5.36}$$

So far, so good? Well, if so, let's break down equation (5.34) to read

$$\%\Delta\varepsilon = \%\Delta P^{US} - \%\Delta P^{ROW}, \tag{5.37}$$

shorthand for which is

$$\hat{\varepsilon} = \hat{P}^{US} - \hat{P}^{ROW}, \tag{5.38}$$

a relationship that goes by the name of *relative purchasing power parity*. If exchange rates can fluctuate, the exchange rate must undergo a percentage change equal to the percentage change in U.S. prices minus the percentage change in rest-of-the-world prices (which is zero in the current example). The U.S. price of a pizza slice rose 100% while the rest-of-the-world price stayed constant. As a result, ε also rose by 100% from 2 to 4.

Now we introduce yet another assumption called the *interest parity condition*:

$$1 + R^{US} = \left(1 + R^{ROW}\right)\left(1 + \hat{\varepsilon}\right), \tag{5.39}$$

where R^{US} is the nominal U.S. interest rate, and R^{ROW} is the nominal rest-of-the-world interest rate. Equation (5.39) is an equilibrium condition, whereby arbitrageurs will move financial capital across national borders in such a way as to equalize the expected nominal return to capital.

Consider an example. Suppose that Eve can buy a bond in Boston for $1,000 and that the interest rate on the bond is 10%. She could also buy a bond in Paris that pays 5%. It seems that the U.S. bond is the better buy. But not so fast. Suppose that Eve expects the dollar to depreciate by 7% before the bond matures in a year. Let's take $\hat{\varepsilon}$ to stand for the expected depreciation of the dollar. Then because ε is the dollar price of a euro, $\hat{\varepsilon}$ equals 7%. So what happens if Eve buys the bond in Paris? Well, if ε equals 2 when she buys the bond, her $1,000 will get her a bond whose face value is €500. At 5%, that bond will pay out €525. But when the bond pays off, those €525 will be worth $1,124, given that a euro now buys $2.14 in American money. She is better off buying the European bond than the American bond, which will pay out only $1,100. Now

$$1 + R^{US} = 1.1 < (1 + R^{ROW})(1 + \hat{\varepsilon}) = 1.124. \tag{5.40}$$

The nominal return to capital in the United States is 10%, while the nominal return to capital in Europe is 12.4%.

This means that money will flow from the United States to Europe, causing R^{ROW} to fall and R^{US} to rise until the two sides of the equation are equal. Conversely, if the U.S. bonds had been the better buy, so that $1 + R$ exceeded $(1 + R^*)(1 + \hat{\varepsilon})$, then money would have moved from Europe to the United States until equation (5.39) was satisfied.

Now we have all the information we need in order to establish the existence of a single, global r. We can simplify equation (5.39) to get

$$R^{US} \approx R^{ROW} + \hat{\varepsilon}, \tag{5.41}$$

whereby the nominal U.S. interest rate will equal the nominal rest-of-the-world (European) interest rate plus the expected depreciation of the dollar. Now substitute equation (5.41) into equation (5.38) to get

$$R^{US} = R^{ROW} + \hat{P}^{US} - \hat{P}^{ROW}, \tag{5.42}$$

which we can rewrite as

$$R^{US} - \hat{P}^{US} = R^{ROW} - \hat{P}^{ROW}. \tag{5.43}$$

Going back to equation (5.22), $R^{US} - \hat{P}^{US} \approx r^{US}$, and $R^{ROW} - \hat{P}^{ROW} \approx r^{ROW}$,
so that

$$r^{US} = r^{ROW} = r. \tag{5.44}$$

If we assume that the depreciation rate is the same everywhere, then

$$cc^{US} = cc^{ROW} = cc. \tag{5.45}$$

Voila! The cost of capital is the same everywhere. We have to distinguish again, however, between intentions and outcomes. For actual r^{US} to equal actual r^{ROW}, lenders and borrowers across the globe must converge on the same expectations of inflation and, from there, the same expectations of currency movements. Also there must be no difference in risk factors that can influence the direction of capital flows.

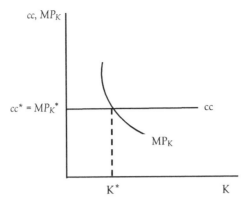

Figure 5.3 The supply and demand for capital in a globalized economy

As far-fetched as these assumptions are, we have to figure that the logic of this discussion has major implications for government policy making. In particular, it implies that policies aimed at increasing domestic saving may have no noticeable effect on domestic investment insofar as increased saving will flow into whatever corner of the globe that offers, momentarily, the highest rate of return. Furthermore, policies aimed specifically at pushing the real domestic interest rate down or up may have no effect because the domestic rate is tied into the global rate.

In this world, the cost of capital line becomes horizontal, and the equilibrium capital stock in any country depends only on where the marginal product of capital curve intersects the cc curve, as in Figure 5.3.

Arnold Harberger once summed this up as follows:

If there is really only one capital market linking most of the economies of the world..., then there is presumably something called a world interest rate, which would become a datum (or exogenous variable) for nearly all of them. A shift of the investment schedule in any such country would simply result in an inflow of funds from the rest of the world—not in a rise in interest rates. An increase in saving, like-wise, would simply spill over the national boundary, and would not result in any change in local interest rates or investment. If, on the other hand, there is little relevance to the concept of a world capital market, then one would expect interest rates in the different countries to be governed by internal factors, being sensitive to shifts in investment and savings, and presumably being influenced by the relative scarcity of capital within each country (Harberger 1980, p. 332).

The Supply and Demand for Labor

Now it's time to take up the question of how wage adjustments equilibrate the supply and demand for labor. In Chapter 3, we worked out the condition under which workers adjust their work time to the real wage they get for their efforts. And we have worked out the condition under which income earners adjust their saving to the return on saving. We have also worked out the condition for matching the saving choices of income-earners with the investment choices of firms.

Now it remains to do two further things: First we have to work out the condition for matching the work choices of individuals with the hiring choices of firms. Second, we have to move beyond the static analyses of previous chapters to take up the conditions for economic growth as they pertain to work and saving. We postpone that discussion to the next chapter.

Let's think again about production in terms of pizza. In fact, let's assume that the only thing the economy produces is pizza. To keep things simple, suppose further that pizza sells for $1 a slice and that the employment of an additional hour of labor permits the firm to produce two more pizzas or 20 more slices.

We say that the marginal product of labor MP_l is the additional amount of production that is forthcoming per additional unit of labor employed or, in this instance,

$$MP_l = \frac{\Delta y}{\Delta l} = \frac{\$20}{1} = \$20. \tag{5.46}$$

If the worker is paid a nominal wage W of $10 per hour, then because the dollar price of a slice of pizza P is 1.00, his real wage w is also $10.

$$w = \frac{W}{P} = \frac{\$10}{1} = \$10. \tag{5.47}$$

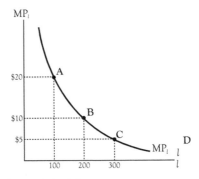

Figure 5.4 The demand for labor curve

The question is how much labor should the firm hire.

Consider Figure 5.4, where the MP_l curve is the demand for labor curve. At point A, the firm is using 100 units of labor per day, at which quantity the MP_l is $20. At point C, where it uses 300 units of labor, MP_l is $5 (the law of diminishing returns pushes down MP_l as the number of workers increases). The pizza shop will want to adjust its use of labor to point B, where the firm is using 200 units of labor and where the real cost of an additional hour of labor just equals the MP_r. At any point to the left of B, the marginal product of labor would exceed the cost of hiring labor, and at any point to the right of B, the cost would exceed the marginal product. Thus B is the profit-maximizing point.

Thus in equilibrium,

$$MP_l = w = \$10. \tag{5.48}$$

Now let's think about how much labor workers want to supply. Suppose that a worker can be expected to provide just eight hours of work per day if he is paid $5.00 per hour. The $5.00 that he would receive for providing the fifth hour is just high enough to compensate for the leisure that he sacrifices for working that hour. Thus his MRS_{LeLay} = $5.00. When he provides 10 hours, his MRS_{LeLay} is $10 and when he provides 15 hours it is $20. If the wage rate is $10, he will provide 10 hours. That is, the reward that he must receive for the last hour of labor provided must just equal the reward that he must receive in order to compensate him for the hour of leisure thus sacrificed. See Figure 5.5.

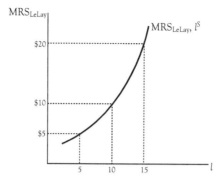

Figure 5.5 *The supply of labor curve*

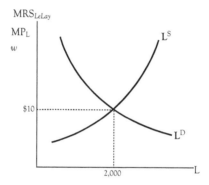

Figure 5.6 *The supply and demand for labor*

Suppose there are 10 firms of the kind described earlier and 200 workers. Figure 5.6 provides the aggregate supply and demand curves that are derived from the foregoing assumptions. In equilibrium, supply and demand bring the MRS_{LeLay} for each worker and the MP_L into line with the real wage rate so that

$$MRS_{LeLay} = MP_L = w. \qquad (5.49)$$

See Figure 5.6.

If w temporarily rises above $10, the quantity of labor supplied will exceed the quantity demanded, and w will fall. If w temporarily falls below $10, the quantity of labor demanded will exceed the quantity supplied, and w will rise. Only when $w = $10, is the labor market in equilibrium.

One More Step

Now let's wrap up this chapter by assuming a particular production function applies to the firm and the economy. A production function that offers convenience and simplicity is the Cobb-Douglas production function, specified as

$$Y = ZK^{\alpha} L^{1-\alpha}, \tag{5.50}$$

where Z stands for *total factor productivity* and is a coefficient that represents the state of existing technology and the general legal and cultural conditions in which business operates. The coefficient α represents the share of income Y going to owners of capital and the coefficient $(1 - \alpha)$ the share going to labor. If we refer to Table 2.7 in Chapter 2, labor compensation was 63% of national income in 2016. If we treat all the other components of national income as income to capital, the capital share was 37%.

When we are using the Cobb-Douglas production function, we can calculate the MP_K and MP_L as follows:

$$MP_K = \frac{\alpha Y}{K}, \tag{5.51}$$

and

$$MP_L = \frac{(1-\alpha)Y}{L}. \tag{5.52}$$

We can therefore write

$$cc = \frac{\alpha Y}{K}, \tag{5.53}$$

and

$$w = \frac{(1-\alpha)Y}{L}. \tag{5.54}$$

This establishes an important link between the return to investing and the ratio of output to capital and between the real wage rate and the ratio of output to labor. Thinking of $\frac{Y}{K}$ as the productivity of capital and $\frac{Y}{L}$ as the productivity of labor, we see the link between productivity and the reward for saving and for work.

With these fundamentals in place, we can now go on to consider the problem of economic growth.

CHAPTER 6

Economic Growth

One of the most important challenges facing policy makers is the question of how to increase economic growth. Developing countries stuck with low living standards strive to overcome centuries of poverty. Developed countries facing an extended economic slump search for an answer as to how to return to "normal" growth.

One of the enduring myths, exposed in vivid detail by William Easterly in his book, *The Elusive Quest for Economic Growth,* is that the path to more rapid growth lies in bringing more investment to bear on the problem (Easterly 2001, p. 4). This is an appealing solution, based as it is in what amounts to a half-truth about the power of investment to propel an economy forward. It is also a misleading solution, as it is based on wishful thinking about the ability of government to manage economic growth through top-down policies.

So what do we want to grow when we try to increase economic growth? The answer must be expressed in terms of measurable aggregates. There is no systematic way to address the problem of national "happiness" under this heading (see Chapter 2). The measurable aggregates that are ordinarily used and that give us a handle on the problem are output, or more specifically, GDP per person and consumption per person.

Let's continue with our practice of using the letter C to stand for aggregate consumption, and let's now let POP stand for population. We can then say that the two most important measures of economic growth are the growth of Y/POP and C/POP. Output per person is important because it provides the broadest measure of economic performance. But economic welfare depends on how much of the output goes to consumption. As Adam Smith said, "consumption is the sole end and purpose of all production." A benevolent dictator might set about doing what he could to maximize the growth of C/POP for his country.

Let's approach the problem of growth by using the model developed by Robert M. Solow (Solow 1956). As we work through this chapter it will be convenient to use population as a proxy for the total number of people employed. It is in fact a pretty good proxy. In April 2000, 64.7% of the U.S. civilian population that was 16 and older had jobs. In December 2017, the number stood at 60.1%. Part of the recent decline is due to the lingering effects of the recession of 2007–2009 and part is the retirement of baby boomers, now in full sway. In discussing growth theory, however, we cannot readily allow for such swings in employment. Here we will talk interchangeably about "population" and "labor," as if the two were the same.

Another convenient, probably necessary, procedure is to treat the quantity of labor L as the number of persons working and to assume that everyone who wants to work is working. There is no recognition of the sensitivity of labor supply to current wages, future wages, and the state of the economy in this assumption. In effect, we assume that the country has reached an equilibrium in which everyone, young and old alike, is working. Fluctuations in the labor-force participation rate are the subject of the next volume, but not this one.

Finally, we assume that the saving rate s is fixed (never mind the extensive discussion in Chapter 4 about how individuals adjust their saving rate according to the parameters r, ρ, and IES). Whatever decisions or "propensities" determine the aggregate saving rate, they are "exogenous" or outside the model we will be using.

Proceeding in this spirit, two ratios become important: the size of the capital stock per person $\dfrac{K}{L}$ and output per person $\dfrac{Y}{L}$. We will begin by focusing on $\dfrac{Y}{L}$.

In the preceding chapter, we established the links between saving and capital formation and between capital formation and production. Let's take the Cobb-Douglas production function, introduced there,

$$Y = ZK^{\alpha} L^{1-\alpha}, \tag{6.1}$$

and divide both sides by L to get

$$\frac{Y}{L} = Z\left[\frac{K}{L}\right]^{\alpha}. \tag{6.2}$$

Reconfigured in terms of economic growth, this equation becomes

$$\%\Delta\frac{Y}{L} = \%\Delta Z + \alpha\%\Delta\left(\frac{K}{L}\right). \qquad (6.3)$$

To grasp the relevance of this equation, imagine that Z doesn't change. Then, if capital and labor are rising at the same rate *and* if Z is constant, the left-hand side of equation (6.3) is zero.

And now we can see a dark and foreboding truth about economic growth: There is a "steady state" of the economy in which K and L are rising at the same rate and in which Y and L are also therefore rising at the same rate. Growth of the kind that everyone wants requires output to rise faster than population. So if the economy reaches a state in which both output and population are rising at the same rate, we have to see the economy as expanding only fast enough to keep living standards at what might well be the same, deplorably low, level.

To see this let's think of what the steady state looks like in an economy in which population is not changing. There is no growth of L.

Observe that the capital stock in any given period equals the capital stock in the previous period, adjusted for depreciation and investment in that period:

$$K_{t+1} = K_t(1 - d) + I_t \qquad (6.4)$$

Because dK_t = depreciation in period t, D_t,

$$I_t = K_{t+1} - K_t + D_t = \Delta K + D_t \qquad (6.5)$$

We know that

$$sY_t = I_t, \qquad (6.6)$$

which is to say that gross saving equals gross investment. In the previous chapter, in which we ignored population and technological change, we found that profit-maximizing firms will reach an equilibrium in which ΔK is zero. When the firm has achieved this equilibrium,

$$sY_t = I_t = D_t. \qquad (6.7)$$

In order to prevent the capital stock from eroding, saving must equal the rate of economic depreciation times the capital stock. To put it differently, once the firm has reached equilibrium, the level of saving is only high enough to prevent the capital stock from eroding. Indeed, it is possible for governments to increase the saving rate s through policies aimed at reducing the cost of capital. And it is true that an increase in the saving rate would then bring about an increase in the demand for capital and a new equilibrium, at a higher capital stock, where the equilibrium (6.7) is satisfied. But note that this would be a once-and-for-all adjustment in K, which would not repeat itself without a further decrease in the cost of capital, and so on.

Now let's keep Z fixed but allow that L is growing at the rate $\hat{L}$. Then

$$L_{t+1} = L_t(1+\hat{L}), \text{ and} \qquad (6.8)$$

$$Y_{t+1} = Y_t(1+\hat{Y}), \qquad (6.9)$$

where $\hat{L}$ is the percentage change in the labor force from one year to the next and $\hat{Y}$ is the percentage change in output from one year to the next.

Let's put some hypothetical numbers on this now. Let:

- $Y_t = \$500,000$,
- $L_t = 100$,
- $s = 20\%$,
- $d = 2\%$,
- $K_t = \$1,000,000$, and
- $\hat{L} = 3\%$.

We note that the *capital-to-labor ratio* in period t is

$$\frac{K_t}{L_t} = \frac{\$1,000,000}{100} = \$10,000, \qquad (6.10)$$

and the *output-to-labor* ratio is

$$\frac{Y_t}{L_t} = \frac{\$500,000}{100} = \$5,000. \qquad (6.11)$$

Whether the capital-to-labor ratio actually falls, rises, or remains the same depends on what's going on with saving. Suppose, for now, that $s = 0$, which is to say that there is no saving in period t. Then the *capital-to-labor ratio* will fall by

$$(\hat{L} + d)\frac{K_t}{L_t} = (0.03 + 0.02)\left(\frac{\$1,000,000}{100}\right) = \$500, \qquad (6.12)$$

from \$10,000 to \$9,500. If the numerator of $\frac{K_t}{L_t}$ falls by 2% because of depreciation and if the denominator rises by 3% because of growth in the labor force, the ratio will fall by 5%.

Now let $s = 20\%$ and consider two scenarios. In the first scenario, saving per person is

$$s\frac{Y_t}{L_t} = 0.2\frac{\$500,000}{100} = \$1,000. \qquad (6.13)$$

Thus,

$$s\frac{Y_t}{L_t} = \$1,000 > (\hat{L} + d)\frac{K_t}{L_t} = \$500, \qquad (6.14)$$

and there is more than enough saving per person to maintain the current capital-to-labor ratio. Hence the capital-to-labor ratio will rise.

Now consider scenario 2, in which the capital-to-labor ratio has tripled so that it equals \$30,000. Under the law of diminishing returns the output-to-labor ratio will rise by less than the capital-to labor ratio. Suppose then that the output-to-labor ratio has risen by 10%, from \$5,000 to \$5,500.

Now

$$s\frac{Y_t}{L_t} = (0.2)\$5,500 = \$1,100 < (\hat{L} + d)\frac{K_t}{L_t} = (0.03 + 0.02)\$30,000 = \$1,500. \quad (6.15)$$

Because saving per person is less than the amount needed to sustain the capital-to-labor ratio, the capital-to-labor ratio must fall.

The economy thus reaches a steady-state equilibrium when

$$s\frac{Y}{L} = (\hat{L} + d)\frac{K}{L}, \tag{6.16}$$

that is, when the capital-to-labor ratio is just high enough that the actual saving per person equals the saving per person needed to keep the capital-to-labor ratio from either rising or falling. In this example, this could be where the capital-to-labor ratio is $21,000 and the output-per-labor ratio is $5,250:

$$s\frac{Y_t}{L_t} = (0.2)\$5,250 = \$1,050$$

$$= (L_g + d)\frac{K_t}{L_t} = (0.03 + 0.02)\$21,000 = \$1,050. \tag{6.17}$$

From this example, we can see that as long as $s, \hat{L}$, and d are fixed, the output-per-labor ratio must remain fixed at $5,250 and the capital-to-labor ratio must remain fixed at $21,000. But if $\hat{L}$ is fixed at 3%, then the growth of output and of capital, $\hat{Y}(= \%\Delta Y)$ and $\hat{K} = (\%\Delta K)$, must also remain fixed at 3%. The economy is said to have reached a "steady state" when the growth of labor, capital, and output, $\hat{L}$, $\hat{K}$, and $\hat{Y}$, are all equal.

Now assume that L, K, and Y are all growing at the same rate. If we go back to equation (6.2), we see that output per worker remains constant if Z remains constant (which we currently assume) and if K and L are rising at the same rate.

This is to be expected, given a Cobb-Douglas production function, which has built into it the assumption that a given percentage change in both labor and capital will yield the same percentage change in output.

From equation (6.1), we know that

$$\%\Delta Y = \%\Delta Z + \alpha(\%\Delta K) + (1 - \alpha)(\%\Delta L). \tag{6.18}$$

Letting $\%\Delta Z = \hat{Z}$,

$$\hat{Y} = \hat{Z} + a\hat{K} + (1 - a)\hat{L}. \tag{6.19}$$

Given that $\widehat{Z} = 0$,

$$\widehat{Y} = \widehat{K} = \widehat{L}. \tag{6.20}$$

We can show graphically how this comes about. See Figure 6.1.

The graph shows different levels of output per person, $\dfrac{Y}{L}$, and saving per person, $s\dfrac{Y}{L}$, for different values of the capital-to-labor ratio, $\dfrac{K}{L}$. The $s\dfrac{Y}{L}$ line cuts the $\left(\widehat{L}+d\right)\dfrac{K}{L}$ line at $\left(\dfrac{K}{L}\right)^{*}$, which tells us that the amount of saving per person needed to sustain the corresponding capital-to-labor ratio is just matched by the amount of saving per person that is forthcoming. For points to the left of $\left(\dfrac{K}{L}\right)^{*}$, $s\dfrac{Y}{L}$ would exceed $\left(\widehat{L}+d\right)\dfrac{K}{L}$ and the capital-to-labor ratio would rise. For points to the right, $\left(\widehat{L}+d\right)\dfrac{K}{L}$ would exceed $s\dfrac{Y}{L}$ and the capital-to-labor ratio would fall. Only where $\left(\dfrac{K}{L}\right) = \left(\dfrac{K}{L}\right)^{*}$, does $s\dfrac{Y}{L} = \left(\widehat{L}+d\right)\dfrac{K}{L}$ and only there is the capital-to-labor ratio constant.

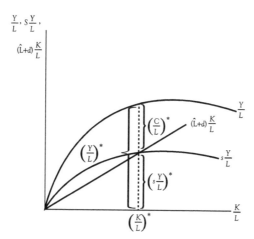

Figure 6.1 The Solow growth model

The capital-labor ratio, $\left(\dfrac{K}{L}\right)^{*}$, is called the *steady state* ratio because

it is just high enough to keep $\dfrac{Y}{L}$ constant. Equation (6.20) holds true when the system is in the steady state. But then, as equation (6.3) implies,

$\%\Delta\dfrac{Y}{L}$ must be zero, meaning that output per capita cannot rise unless Z is rising. More generally

$$\%\Delta\frac{Y}{L} = \%\Delta Z. \qquad (6.21)$$

The only way to bring about growth of per-capita output is to bring about growth of Z.

What Is Needed to Spur Growth

What is needed for per-capita output to grow? There are two portals through which government can exert its influence. Government can directly affect s by instituting policies that either encourage or discourage saving. The other portal, its influence on Z, is harder to pin down. (Because the growth of the labor force is considered fixed here, we ignore the influence government can have over the supply and demand for labor.)

Suppose that the economic planners, or government officials responsible for tax policy as it affects s, decide to cut taxes on saving in order to increase s. The $s\dfrac{Y}{L}$ line rotates upward in a counterclockwise direction, pushing the economy up along the $\left(\hat{L}+d\right)\dfrac{K}{L}$ line, to a new steady-state capital-to-labor ratio, $\left(\dfrac{K}{L}\right)^{*'}$.

What has this action accomplished? Well, it has brought about a once-and-for all increase in output per capita (a higher ratio of Y to L). But once the capital-to-labor ratio reaches $\left(\dfrac{K}{L}\right)^{*'}$, the economy settles back into a steady state, in which, K, L, and Y are all rising at the same rate as they were before the increase in s. Output per person is higher than it was at $\left(\dfrac{K}{L}\right)^{*}$, but the growth of output per person experienced during the transition to this higher capital-to-labor ratio comes to a halt.

This might seem to imply that the government could keep pushing the economy further up the $\dfrac{Y}{L}$ curve just by taking steps to increase s. That, however, is neither practical nor desirable. A country that combines political with economic freedom will not respond, beyond a certain point, to government policies aimed at increasing the saving rate. Taxes on the return to saving are a deterrent to saving but if all such taxes were removed there would be little left in the government policy arsenal to encourage further saving. Even under a command economy, political resistance to ever-higher "forced saving" would put practical limits on this policy. After all, people will not tolerate a state of affairs in which the government compels them to save 100% of their income.

Insofar as it is government policy to maximize consumption per person, there does exist a theoretically ideal saving rate. To see this, observe that the marginal product of capital measures the increase in output that results from adding another dollar to the stock of capital, while holding labor constant. Suppose that the capital-to-labor ratio is at $\left(\dfrac{K}{L}\right)^{*}$ in Figure 6.1, so that the condition $s\dfrac{Y}{L}=\left(\hat{L}+d\right)\dfrac{K}{L}$ is satisfied. But suppose also that MP_{K}, given by the slope of $\dfrac{Y}{L}$, is 6% but that $\hat{L}+d$ equals 5%. Whereas saving per person is just high enough to preserve the existing ratio of capital to labor, the government could notch up consumption per person by pushing up the saving rate.

Let's see why. Under our assumptions, it is necessary to add only 5 cents to output per person to sustain the capital-to-labor ratio if that ratio rises by one dollar. But if MP_{K} = 0.06, the rise in the ratio will add 6 cents to output. Where would the other 1 cent go? The answer is to consumption. (Note that in this world $C + S = C + I = Y$, so every dollar of Y that does not go to S or therefore I must go to C.) Thus a policy aimed at increasing the saving rate (and therefore moving further up the $\left(\hat{L}+d\right)\dfrac{K}{L}$ curve) would, for a while at least, increase consumption per person. In the steady state in Figure 6.1, the consumption-to-labor ratio is $\left(\dfrac{C}{L}\right)^{*}$. An increase in the saving rate under these circumstances would increase $\left(\dfrac{C}{L}\right)$ to a higher level.

Now consider another steady state, this one reached at $\left(\dfrac{K}{L}\right)^{*'}$. Here, we assume that MP_K is only 4%, the law of diminishing returns having operated in its ineluctable way. Now think about the *last* dollar added to the capital stock (per unit of labor). That dollar increased output per person by only 4%, whereas it is necessary for 5% of output to go to saving and investment in order to sustain the capital-to-labor ratio at this level. The missing 1% must come out of consumption. So now to increase consumption-per person, the s should fall to bring $\dfrac{K}{L}$ down into line with some intermediate capital-to-labor ratio, $\left(\dfrac{K}{L}\right)_{GR}$, at which

$$MP_K = \hat{L} + d. \tag{6.22}$$

Given the Cobb-Douglas function, this would mean that

$$\frac{aY}{K} = \hat{L} + d. \tag{6.23}$$

Equation (6.22) is called the *golden rule* for economic growth, in that, by satisfying it, the economy maximizes current consumption per person. The saving rate is brought just high enough so that any other steady-state capital-to-labor ratio would yield a lower level of consumption per capita. This designation might not quite fit the meaning behind the Biblical golden rule, insofar as it might be godlier for the current generation to save for the purpose of lifting the next generation's standard of living. Yet, the idea is clear. The thus-stated golden rule has a degree of moral authority in that it puts individual welfare ahead of some central authority that might wish to distinguish itself by forcing growth on the current generation to create a kind of shrine to its command-and-control efforts. See Stalinist Russia.

This line of thought reminds us, though, of the limited scope of efforts to influence the saving rate for the purpose of increasing economic growth. An increase in the saving rate will increase output per person but, once the new steady state is attained, it will not increase the growth of output per person.

This leaves us with the hope to influence Z. Returning to equation (6.3), assume that the economy is in a steady state, so that $\%\Delta\left(\dfrac{K}{L}\right)$ is zero. Now suppose that, through either public or private initiatives, Z rises by

2% annually. Then $\dfrac{Y}{L}$ will also rise by 2% annually. This observation points to a truth that is both powerful and daunting, that is, that living standards will steadily improve with technical progress (as well as other kinds of progress associated with Z) but will only temporarily improve without such progress.

This should be seen as a cautionary tale on the matter of economic growth. This book argues that government can expand work and saving, and therefore output, by reducing taxes on work and saving. But a necessary condition for growth in living standards, as measured by output per capita, is steady growth in *total factor productivity, Z,* combined with the institutional and legal environment that is needed to encourage innovation and entrepreneurship.

Gordon on the Decline of Growth

There is currently a lot of pessimism on the prospects for U.S. economic growth. Figure 6.2 shows that the growth of total factor productivity has fallen sharply since 2010, after generally rising over the period 1996 to 2004. In 2016, the macroeconomist Robert J. Gordon published a massive volume titled *The Rise and Fall of American Growth,* in which he concluded that various "headwinds" are causing growth to fall. He predicted that "future growth in the disposable income of the bottom 99 percent of the income distribution... is likely to be barely positive and substantially lower than the growth of the labor productivity [output per man hour] of the total economy" (Gordon 2016, pp. 530–31).

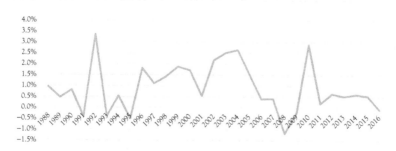

Figure 6.2 Growth of U.S. total factor productivity 1988–2016

Source: U.S. Bureau of Labor Statistics.

Gordon predicts that the annual growth in labor productivity will be 1.2 percent over the next 35 years (compared to 2.71 percent from 1948 to 1970 and 1.38 percent from 1970 to 2015). Output per person will grow by 0.8 percent annually (compared to 2.41 percent from 1920 to 1970 and 1.77 percent from 1970 to 2014) (Gordon 2016, pp. 635, 637).

Gordon identifies three industrial revolutions through which the United States has passed:

1. "Steam, railroads" (1750 to 1830),
2. "Electricity, internal combustion engine, running water, indoor toilets, communications, entertainment, chemicals, petroleum" (1870–1900), and
3. "Computers, the web, mobile phones" (1960–present) (Gordon 2012).

He questions why the last of these has failed "to maintain productivity growth at a faster pace," as shown in the declining productivity in recent years (Gordon 2012, p. 12). One answer, he believes, lies in the trend toward products such as smartphones and iPods, which have served mainly to enhance the lives of consumers, but away from labor-saving innovations (Gordon 2012, p. 13).

Despite the potential for productivity gains offered by artificial intelligence and by methods of extracting information from "big data," future economic growth will be buffeted by six headwinds: "demography, education, inequality, globalization, energy/environment, and the overhang of consumer and government debt" (Gordon 2012).

The demographic trend affecting growth is the reduction in work hours resulting from the retirement of the baby boomers. As for education, "the U.S. is steadily slipping down the international league tables in the percentage of its population of a given age which has completed higher education" (Gordon 2012, p. 16).

Gordon reports that the top one percent of households experienced 52 percent of the growth in real income over the period 1993 to 2008. This trend toward inequality is, in his view, "the most important quantitatively in holding down the growth of our future income" (Gordon 2012, p. 17). The remaining factors are the decline in U.S. wages owing to outsourcing and imports from low-wage countries, the threat of a carbon tax aimed at global warming, and the growing volume of household and government debt (Gordon 2012, pp. 17, 18).

Gordon's pessimism is countered by Michael Mandel and Bret Swanson in a paper that stresses the as-yet unexploited potential of artificial intelligence. "The pessimism about growth," say Mandel and Swanson, "ignores the fact that information has revolutionized only 30% of the private-sector economy. Applying the power of information to the remaining 70% will replicate the gains of digital industries, but on a much larger scale" (Mandel and Swanson 2017, p. 30).

Indeed, everything, considered, Gordon is unpersuasive in his attempt to tie declining productivity to inequality and other factors that have nothing to do with the act of bringing ideas to the marketplace and realizing the potential for increased profits through the introduction of new products and production methods. Inequality is a growing concern among economists, but it has nothing to do with the ability to innovate in a society that respects property rights.

Secular Stagnation

In his March 1939 presidential address before the American Economic Association, Alvin Hansen raised his concerns over "secular stagnation," which he defined as "sick recoveries which die in their infancy and depressions that feed on themselves and leave a hard and seemingly immovable core of unemployment" (Hansen 1939). Hansen spoke when the U.S. economy was recovering from a two-year plunge in real GDP, after having recovered somewhat from the worst of the Great Depression. Prior to the Great Depression, less than full employment was a passing feature of the business cycle.

> Not until the problem of full employment of our productive resources from the long-run, secular standpoint was upon us, were we compelled to give serious consideration to those factors and forces in our economy which tend to make business recoveries weak and anemic and which tend to prolong and deepen the course of depressions. This is the essence of secular stagnation— sick recoveries which die in their infancy and depressions which feed on themselves and leave a hard and seemingly immovable core of unemployment (Hansen 1939, p. 4).

Sounding much like Gordon, Hansen compared the contemporary (1939) U.S. economy unfavorably with the 19th century. The relatively fast economic growth experienced in the earlier period was due in large part to population growth:

> Population growth was itself responsible for a part of the rise in per capita real income, and this, via the influence of a rising consumption upon investment, stimulated capital formation. Thus it is quite possible that population growth may have acted both directly and indirectly to stimulate the volume of capital formation (Hansen 1939, p. 9).

The problem, as Hansen saw it, was the declining birth rate seen in the twentieth century. This, in light of the experience of the previous century, could be expected to suppress private investment, with consequent negative effects on economic growth. The problem for his own generation, said Hansen, "is, above all, the problem of inadequate private investment outlets. What we need is not a slowing down in the progress of science and technology, but rather an acceleration of that rate" (Hansen 1939, p. 10).

What is most interesting about Hansen's article is that, as a leading exponent of Keynesian economics, Hansen expressed his concern that the expansion of government would arise as an obstacle to the investment and innovation. "Can a rising public debt," he asked,

> be serviced by a scheme of taxation which will not adversely affect the marginal return on new investment or the marginal cost of borrowing? Can any tax system, designed to increase the propensity to consume by means of a drastic change in income distribution, be devised which will not progressively encroach on private investment?
>
> From the standpoint of the workability of the system of free enterprise, there emerges the problem of sovereignty in democratic countries confronted in their internal economies with powerful groups—entrepreneurial and wage-earning—which have robbed the price system of that impersonal and non-political character idealized in the doctrine of laissez-faire. It remains still to be seen whether political democracy can in the end survive the disappearance of the automatic price system (Hansen 1939, pp. 12–13).

For Hansen, the danger lay in "vastly enlarged government activities" (Hansen 1939, p. 15). It is useful to observe, in this context, that current government spending in the United States was 16% of GDP in 1939 and is now 33% of GDP.

Now, almost 80 years later, the same threat looms over the U.S. economy. In a recent speech, Larry Summers opined as follows: "Six years ago, macroeconomics was primarily about the use of monetary policy to reduce the already small amplitude of fluctuations about a given trend, while maintaining price stability. That was the preoccupation" (Summers 2014, p. 65). "Today," Summers continued, "we *wish* for the problem of minimizing fluctuations around a satisfactory trend." Continuing, he said, "It is increasingly clear that the trend in growth can be adversely affected over the longer term by what happens in the business cycle" (Summers 2014, pp. 65, 66).

The problem, as Summers described it, is "secular stagnation, the idea that the economy re-equilibrates; hysteresis, the shadow cast forward on economic activity by adverse cyclical developments; and the significance of the zero lower bound for the relative efficacy of monetary and fiscal policy" (Summers 2014, p. 66).

Summers observed that, five years into the recovery from the Great Contraction of 2007 to 2009, actual real GDP was still well below potential real GDP. In particular, the employment-population ratio was still well below the historical norm. The culprit, said Summers, was not total factor productivity (Z in our model) but a lack of investment. For Summers, the principal problem is the declining real interest rate (the rate that equilibrates the supply and demand for capital). The source of the problem is declining population growth and investment, combined with rising saving. With actual nominal interest rates already near zero, there is little to be gained from further reductions in real interest rates. The answer, argued Summers, is for government to undertake a policy of increasing aggregate demand through increased deficit spending. We will have more to say about this idea in Volume II.

Piketty's Laws of Capitalism

Thomas Piketty became world famous in 2014 with the publication of his book, *Capital in the Twenty-First Century*. The book provides a lengthy and fact-filled argument that capitalist countries are characterized by growing income inequality. Among his suggested cures for this unwanted trend are a "global tax on capital" and the imposition of a marginal tax rate of 80 percent on U.S. incomes of $500,000 to $1,000,000 a year (Piketty 2014, pp. 513, 515–39). Because Piketty's book has received widespread attention and approval and because the argument here is that taxes, particularly taxes on capital, suppress economic activity, it is necessary to give his book consideration.

Piketty's book and its title suggest that he reckons himself as a modern successor to Karl Marx, whose *Capital* provided the intellectual foundation for communism. Like Marx, Piketty sees capitalism as governed by certain fundamental laws that presage growing concentration of wealth and power on the part of capitalists, with "terrifying" consequences for democracy and social justice. Piketty's book is very readable, and he makes his point with a few simple formulas. Because his formulas have become widely quoted, let's write them down using his notation. He postulates two "fundamental laws of capitalism" and then a "central contradiction" of capitalism. These are as follows:

- The first fundamental law of capitalism: $\alpha = r \times \beta$.
- The second fundamental law of capitalism: $\beta = s/g$.
- The central contradiction of capitalism: $r > g$.

The first and second fundamental laws are not laws at all and are not limited in their applicability to capitalist economies. They are, rather, truisms that apply to any economy and which fall out of the growth model presented previously. As for the variables in his system:

- For Piketty, as for this book, α is the share of income Y that goes to capital.
- For Piketty, r is average rate of return on capital. In this book we use r to connote both the market discount rate and the average return to capital.
- For Piketty, β is the ratio of the capital stock to income or $\dfrac{K}{Y}$.
- Piketty uses g to denote the growth rate of national income, here denoted $\widehat{Y}$.
- Piketty's s is the ratio of net saving to income, whereas our s is the ratio of gross saving to income.
  - Thus, for Piketty, $s = \dfrac{(S - dK)}{Y}$,

o whereas, in this book, $s = \dfrac{S}{Y}$.

In the forgoing sections of this book, the share of income going to capital is

$$\alpha = r \times \frac{K}{Y}, \tag{6.24}$$

consistent with Piketty's first law.

We can rewrite his second law as

$$\frac{K}{Y} = \frac{\dfrac{S - dK}{Y}}{\hat{Y}}, \tag{6.25}$$

or

$$\hat{Y} = \frac{S - dK}{Y} \frac{Y}{K}. \tag{6.26}$$

Then, as in the Solow model,

$$\hat{Y} = \frac{\Delta K}{K_t}, \text{which is to say,} \tag{6.27}$$

$$\hat{Y} = \hat{K} \tag{6.28}$$

in the steady state.

One might think that Piketty's central contradiction of capital would follow from his fundamental laws, but this is not the case. To see why, let's revert to his notation and insert his second law into his first to get

$$r = g\frac{\alpha}{s}. \tag{6.29}$$

It turns out that his central contradiction ($r > g$) holds only if

$$\frac{\alpha}{s} > 1. \tag{6.30}$$

Suppose, for example that $\alpha = 0.3$ and $s = 0.2$. Then, if $r = 0.05$ (which Piketty takes as a reasonable assumption), $g = 0.033$. Thus $r > g$.

But this example does not, in and of itself, imply increasing inequality. Rather, we can say only (1) that the economy will settle into its steady state and (2) that the saving rate and therefore the capital-to-output ratio would have to rise in order for the economy to reach the golden-rule capital-to-labor ratio.

To understand point (1), return to Piketty's second law, using our notation:

$$\frac{K}{Y} = \frac{\frac{sY - dK}{Y}}{\hat{Y}}. \tag{6.31}$$

Substituting $\hat{L}$ for $\hat{Y}$,

$$sY - dK = K \times \hat{L}. \tag{6.32}$$

Dividing by L,

$$\frac{sY}{L} - \frac{dK}{L} = \frac{K}{L} \times \hat{L}, \tag{6.33}$$

or

$$\frac{sY}{L} = (\hat{L} + d)\frac{K}{L}, \tag{6.34}$$

which is the condition for achieving the steady-state growth of labor, capital, and income as derived in the Solow model.

To understand the second point, as noted previously, recall the golden rule condition for the optimal capital-to-labor ratio:

$$MP_K = \hat{L} + d \tag{6.35}$$

or

$$MP_K - d = \hat{L}. \tag{6.36}$$

From equation (5.25) in Chapter 5, the firm maximizes profit by setting

$$r = MP_K - d. \tag{6.37}$$

If

$$MP_K - d > \hat{L}, \tag{6.38}$$

the golden rule is not satisfied. Then also

$$r > \hat{L}, \tag{6.39}$$

and, because $\hat{Y} = \hat{L}$,

$$r > \hat{Y} \tag{6.40}$$

as in Piketty's "central contradiction."

But equation (6.40) means only that the saving rate is too low to achieve the golden-rule capital-to-labor ratio. Society needs to increase the saving rate and therefore the capital-to-labor ratio in order to maximize consumption per capita.

Piketty devotes some space to a consideration of this reality (Piketty 2014, pp. 562–65), concluding that any suggestion to achieve the golden-rule capital-to-labor ratio is "not very useful in practice" (Piketty 2014, p. 563). Piketty is certainly correct in saying that we cannot usefully set our sights on maximizing consumption per capita. All we can do, in practice, is aim for ways to increase output per capita since we don't have the policy tools to align the marginal product of capital with the sum of population growth and depreciation. The question, again, is what any of this has to do with income inequality.

The answer is, "Nothing at all." In the Solow model presented previously,

$$\hat{Y} = \hat{L} = \hat{K} \tag{6.41}$$

in the steady state. Given the return to capital r and the wage rate w, both capital income (rK) and labor income wL will rise at the same rate as total income, $(rK + wL)$, no matter what the value of r and $\hat{Y}$. If, as Piketty assumes, the share of income going to capital (a) is a given, then so also is the share going to labor $(1 - a)$, and that share is independent of the relationship between r and $\hat{Y}$.

Piketty believes, and provides strong support for his argument, that income inequality is on the rise. He speculates that the trend toward increased inequality is strong and permanent. The question is what his "central contradiction of capitalism" has to do with this, given that it is neither a contradiction nor an inherent feature of capitalism. Indeed, he could have skipped the entire theoretical edifice on which his book hangs and simply focused on the growing literature on labor's declining share of income (Lee and Jayadev 2005; Karabarbounis and Neiman 2013; Rodriguez and Jayadev 2010). One can make an argument that labor is losing out to capital because of capital-augmenting innovation, without resorting to purposeless theorizing.

It is interesting that Piketty devotes some space in his book to squaring Marx's central contradiction with his own (Piketty 2014, pp. 227–30). For Marx, capitalism was doomed because r would steadily fall as the capital-to-labor ratio rose, driving capitalists to ever-more frantic efforts to raise their profit rates—these including wars for new territory and efforts to push down wages—thus ineluctably driving capitalism to collapse. This contradicts Piketty's central contradiction that r is high and rising. One can only wonder why, considering Marx's take on the death spiral affecting capitalism, Piketty sees a connection between his warnings about capitalism and Marx's.

CHAPTER 7

Taxes and the Macroeconomy

Economists have a reputation for disagreeing among themselves, a state of affairs that some believe to disqualify them from commenting on anything. In fact, there are many propositions on which economists generally agree, if only implicitly. One is the law of diminishing returns. You cannot, as someone has pointed out, grow all the world's wheat in a single flower pot. Presumably, also, no one would advocate raising the minimum wage to $100 an hour.[1]

There is another proposition that can't be doubted, and that is, at some point a further increase in the tax rate on whatever is being taxed will cause the government to bring in less revenue rather than more. The school dubbed "supply-side economics" has stressed this principle and correctly so. If the government taxed income at 100%, it would collect no revenue because either no one would bother to earn income or anyone who did would not report any income. This is not "voodoo economics," as President George H. W. Bush called it, to his eternal discredit, but economics you can believe in (Romer and Romer 2010).

Of course, not even the most zealous progressive would advocate a $100 minimum wage or a 100% tax on income, but even less zealous progressives have to own up to an inconvenient (for them) truth, which is that as tax rates rise the base on which a tax is assessed (e.g., income) will ultimately shrink and that, as the tax rate approaches 100%, revenues will shrink to zero. Let t stand for the average tax rate on income. Then tax revenue (TR) in our version of NIPA accounting can be expressed as

---

[1] Senator Elizabeth Warren of Massachusetts did once suggest that the minimum wage should be $22 an hour. See Senator Elizabeth Warren, "Minimum Wage Would Be $22 An Hour If It Had Kept Up With Productivity," 2013. Retrieved August 18, 2013, from http://huffingtonpost.com/2013/03/18/elizabeth-warren-minimum-wage_n_2900984.html

$$TR = tY(t). \tag{7.1}$$

This reminds us that in the real world of tax policy, the amount of tax revenue collected by government equals the tax rate applied to some tax base (here, income) and that the tax base itself depends on the rate at which it is taxed.

It takes only a little math to illustrate this point. Let Y (here, income or GDP) be the tax base, as measured to reflect the effect of t on Y, and let t be the rate at which income is taxed. We can then say that total tax revenue TR is simply the product of t and Y.

We can use this equation to compute the percentage change in revenue that results from a given percentage change in t as

$$\%\Delta TR = \%\Delta t + \%\Delta Y. \tag{7.2}$$

To hear some progressives talk about tax policy, $\%\Delta Y$ is always zero or close to it. This is to say that if the tax rate goes up by 10% so will revenues. Thus government can make the tax rate as high as it wants without worrying that income, and eventually also tax revenues, will start to fall. When you hear people talk about "static" revenue estimates, this is what they mean. Such estimates presuppose a zero taxpayer response to any tax-law change. A given percentage increase in the tax rate always yields an equal percentage increase in revenues. That any policy maker or policy advisor would endorse such a principle is bewildering but true.

Static estimates belong in the same category as arguments about getting all the world's wheat out of a single flower pot or raising the minimum wage to $100 an hour. Plausibly, when the tax rate is very low, a rise in the tax rate would have little effect on Y or might even, because of the income effect, cause Y to rise. But imagine that you are a worker making $50 an hour and already paying 75% of your hour wage in taxes, only to learn that now the government wants to collect 85%. Currently, the sacrifice of another hour of leisure lets you take home only an additional $12.50. Now the government wants you to take home only $7.50. At some point in this process you will surely discover that your time is better used in such untaxable pursuits as growing your own food or earning your income under the table.

If the government doesn't want to collect any tax revenue on income, it just sets t to zero. But it is inevitable that as t rises, Y will at some point shrink, that is, %ΔY will become negative. Once Y starts to shrink, the effect of an increase in t on REV depends on how much %ΔY offsets %Δt. At some point, that sensitivity will be so high that further increases in t will cause revenues to fall, that is, the numerical value of %ΔY will exceed that of %Δt.

The Laffer Curve

This leads us to the famous Laffer curve, which, by legend, economist Arthur Laffer drew on a cocktail napkin for Congressman Jack Kemp at a DC restaurant. (Jack Kemp took the "supply-side" ideas he got from Laffer to Congress where he cosponsored what became the Reagan tax cuts.) The napkin is lost to history, but Figure 7.1 provides a version of what Laffer drew.

The drawing captures the fact that when tax rates are low, in the region of t_1, further increases in the tax rate will bring about an increase in revenue. But when tax rates are high, in the region of t_2, it is reductions in the tax that will bring about an increase in revenue. Perforce there must be some tax rate, t^{MAX} that will yield the most amount of revenue TR^{MAX}. The curve is tilted to the right in Figure 7.1 to reflect the apparent fact that in most instances the tax rate would have exceeded 50% before further increases t would yield declining revenues.

The argument that government could increase revenues by cutting the tax rate is also, however, too easily made. "Supply-siders" too often make this argument. The reality is that tax rates will usually be closer to t_1 than to t_2 along the horizontal axis of Figure 7.1, so that a cut in the tax rate will cause revenue to fall. On the other hand, anti-supply-siders too often

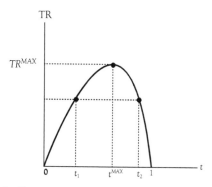

Figure 7.1 The Laffer curve

claim that a rise in the tax rate will bring about a proportional rise in revenues, which also is almost never true. As stated, a rational approach to tax policy takes it as a given that government must raise a certain amount of revenue and that the goal is to raise that revenue with minimum damage to the economy, in this simple example, with minimum shrinkage in Y.

It is important, in studying Figure 7.1, to keep in mind that t^{MAX} is not necessarily the optimal t. The optimal t will balance out the benefits that a further rise in t would confer against the costs that it would impose. Imagine that the government has set t at t_1 and that it is considering a small rise in t. The question is whether the value of the additional government spending made possible by that rise in t would more than offset the harm inflicted by the resulting fall in Y. If not, then it should not raise t. Conversely, it should consider whether the good made possible through the resulting rise in Y would more than offset the harm, through reduced government spending, of a reduction in t. If so, then it should reduce t. Only if neither a rise nor a fall in t is called for, on that line of thinking, has the government imposed the optimal t.

It is important to keep one more point in mind as we proceed. That point is that there is a huge difference between two kinds of tax law changes: those that affect the reward for choosing work over leisure or for choosing saving over consumption, on the one hand, and those that simply make the taxpayer poorer or richer, on the other. Probably the best examples of tax changes that exerted little influence on the rewards for work or saving were the tax rebates that were sent out under the administration of George W. Bush for the purpose of stimulating the economy.

If the government sends you a check in the mail, it can call that a tax rebate but it has exactly the same effect on your work–leisure decision or your saving–consumption decision that would occur if you received a lottery winning or a distribution from the estate of your late Aunt Edna whom you never knew very well. It just makes you richer without affecting the reward for putting another hour into work or another dollar into saving.

A check in the mail or any economic windfall produces a pure "income effect" of the kind discussed in Chapter 3. Although economic windfalls do affect the work–saving calculus, they do not affect it by making work or saving more or less attractive relative to leisure or consumption "at the margin." They do not affect the reward for choosing another hour of work over another hour of leisure or for choosing another dollar of saving over another dollar of consumption. In other words, they do not exert substitution effects. They simply make current leisure and current consumption look more attractive.

Conversely, if the individual gets a bill in the mail for some amount of money that is unrelated to his reward for working another hour or saving another dollar, it affects his work–saving calculus only by making him feel poorer. The bill makes current leisure or consumption less attractive.

In Volume II, Chapter 3, we will see that the effects of tax changes under nonclassical conditions—say, a prolonged period of low production and employment—depend on how those conditions came about. Because there is a long-standing assumption that an economic downturn reflects general excess supply and because Keynes predicated his economic remedies on that assumption, tax rebates are often seen to be appropriate whenever the economy falls into a prolonged downturn. But we will see that an economy can fall into a prolonged downturn for reasons opposite of what Keynes assumed—say, for reasons stemming from general excess demand—and that the provision of economic windfalls through tax rebates may therefore be exactly the wrong remedy.

In this chapter we assume the existence of classical conditions, under which a gain or loss of cash, separate from any change in the reward for work or saving, exerts an income effect and that this income effect is registered under conditions in which aggregate supply equals aggregate demand. We will proceed on the assumption that there is no Keynesian excess supply or, conversely, any suppressed-inflation type excess demand, to worry about. We relax these assumptions in Volume II.

Tax laws exert many effects on behavior beyond their direct income effects. Take a look at your IRS Form 1040. If you subtracted "education expenses" to compute your adjusted gross income, then the availability of that deduction probably influenced your education spending. The deduction for "alimony" paid might even affect your decision to get divorced or not (which one can hope you didn't have to do). Other items (deductions for student loan interest, charitable expenses, and personal exemptions) influenced other choices, which, presumably, they were intended to do. Some of these features of the law do impose substitution effects but these are so hard to separate from their income effects as to make it difficult to fit them into an analysis of how tax law affects the overall economy. It is therefore useful, in studying macroeconomics, simply to treat such deductions as if they were just "checks in the mail," every bit the same as tax rebates.

Our job here is to understand how tax changes affect the economy and to do so by understanding how they affect decisions to supply and use labor and capital. We begin by considering labor.

Taxes on Labor Income

Recall the discussion of substitution and income effects in Chapter 3, which we have considered in Figure 7.2. In this example, Adam saw his wage rise from $50 to $100 per hour, only to have his boss extort $500 in income from him as his wage rose. There we saw that Adam would allocate more time to work at the new wage rate if he had to pay this extortion than if he did not. The extortion took away the income effect that would otherwise have led Adam to consume more leisure.

Now let's approach this situation from the other way around, and let's let the government take on the role of Adam's boss. Adam starts out by working 12 hours a day and making $100 per hour in labor income. Then the government imposes a 50% tax on his income so that his after-tax

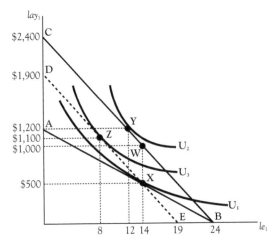

Figure 7.2 *Effect of a tax on labor income*

wage rate falls to $50 per hour. He increases leisure by two hours from 12 to 14 hours per day, reducing his work from 12 to 10 hours per day. Of the $1,000 in before-tax income that he now earns, he pays $500 to the government, leaving the rest in after-tax labor income. His utility falls from U_2 to U_1.

The adjustment in his work effort is the product of competing substitution and income effects. Because his after-tax wage rate falls by 50%, the cost of leisure also falls by 50% and Adam, to that extent, wants more leisure. But he must also pay $500 in taxes on his $1,000 in before-tax income, as shown by point W, which means that he can afford less leisure than before. The income effect on work and leisure results from the downward shift of $500 by the budget line from BC to DE and the shift from point Y to point Z. The substitution effect is illustrated by the shift from point Z to point X. Adam reduces his leisure time (and increases his work time) by four hours because of the income effect and increases his leisure time (and decreases his work time) by six hours because of the substitution effect. The net expansion in leisure time (and contraction of work time) by two hours is the net result of these competing effects.

In this example, the work-increasing income effect of the tax offsets much of the work-decreasing substitution effect. It seems, in light of this example, that a tax on labor income might cause only a small reduction in the supply of labor. Conversely, the removal or reduction of a tax on labor income might cause only a small increase in labor supply.

The discussion of Chapter 3 brings another point to light. Suppose that the government decided to collect its $500, not by taxing labor income, but by simply sending Adam a bill for $500, which he would have to pay irrespective of his work–leisure choice. It imposes what we call a *lump-sum tax*. This would be akin to the hypothesized "donation" that his boss expected him to make in the example of that chapter. After he pays the government, Adam gets to keep the entire $100 in pay that he receives for every hour he works.

As in Chapter 3, we illustrate that eventuality by a shift inward of his budget constraint from BC to ED. This action eliminates the substitution effect since it leaves take-home pay (once the tax bill is paid) unchanged. The cost of leisure does not go down and as a result there is no inclination on that account to substitute leisure for work. All that is left is the income effect, which, since Adam feels poorer now than he did at point Y, induces him to reduce his leisure from 12 to 8 hours (and increase his work from 12 to 16 hours) as he shifts from point Y to point Z. There is an argument from the economic efficiency viewpoint to go from the existing tax system to a more neutral tax under which income effects replace substitution effects in this manner. Adam is better off at point Z than he would be at point X. It also happens that his work time rises by four hours rather than falling by two hours as it does under the income tax.

Interestingly, this argument flies in the face of the "folk-economic" view that the harm from taxes results from the fact that they "take money out of people's pockets." But the harm is greater under an income tax than under a lump-sum tax. Either tax takes the same amount of money out of the taxpayer's pockets, but the income tax imposes an additional harm by reducing the cost of leisure and thereby inducing the taxpayer to increase leisure, in which case he ends up worse off than he would have been under a lump-sum tax.

We reach the conclusion that the economic effect of a tax depends on just how it is assessed. But it also depends on how government uses the tax revenue it raises. The forgoing analysis disregards this question entirely. It assumes, in effect, that that government takes $500 of Adam's money—money that would otherwise have gone toward the purchase of useful consumer goods—and applies it to some entirely wasteful project. Perhaps the government pays workers to dig holes in the ground and fill them in again, diverting those workers from the production of previously enjoyed consumer goods. (Oddly, this possibility would work just fine in an economy characterized by Keynesian excess supply, but recall that we are assuming that there is no imbalance between aggregate supply and demand.)

Figure 7.3 illustrates an alternative scenario, one in which the individual is subjected to a 50% income tax but nevertheless rises to a higher level of utility because of the value to him of the government services paid for out of the tax revenue raised by the tax. Suppose that service is the provision of "free" health care, for which Adam previously paid $600 out of his pocket. This can be thought of as a lump-sum benefit, which Adam gets without doing anything at all. This tax-benefit combination puts him on line EF. This line is based on the assumption that Adam can enjoy the $600 in consumption without working at all (point E). At the

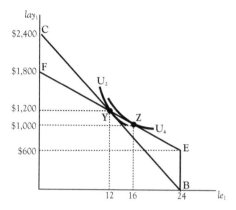

Figure 7.3 Effect of an income tax when tax revenue is not wasted

other extreme, he could enjoy $1,800 in consumption by working the entire 24 hours (point F).

Now also Adam can have the same amount of consumption and the same amount of leisure that he had before the tax-benefit arrangement was instituted, which means that it permits him to return to point Y, where he has 12 hours of leisure and $1,200 in consumption and the same level of utility U_2. In actuality, because the tax makes leisure cheaper, he would adjust to point Z and to a higher level of utility U_4.

Interestingly now, the government raises less in revenue than it did when it wasted the money, the reason being that the $600 windfall partially offsets the income effect of the income tax, causing him to expand leisure by two hours more than he would have if the revenue had been wasted. Thus, he ends up working only eight hours and paying only $400 in taxes. His eight hours of work leaves him with $400 in after-tax income, which, plus the value of the government benefit, permits him to consume $1,000 worth of goods. (Keep in mind that, in this example, it must be possible for the government to provide the aimed-for $600 in services by raising only $400 in revenue.)

These examples relate to taxes on labor income, but they apply as well to taxes on capital income. They teach three lessons:

1. Income taxes that are applied to the provision of wasteful government projects generate offsetting substitution and income effects

with corresponding offsetting effects on the supply of the activity that is being taxed (e.g., the supply of labor).

2. Insofar as it is possible to replace an income tax with a more neutral, lump-sum tax (and whether or not the revenue is spent on wasteful projects), government will raise revenues in a fashion that eliminates substitution effects and leaves only income effects. This will result in an increase in the activity (for example work) that was previously taxed and an increase in individual welfare.

3. When the government imposes an income tax and applies the tax revenue it collects to the benefit of the worker through useful spending projects, it creates a positive income effect that offsets the negative income effect of the tax itself. If the benefit provided by the expenditure exceeds the amount of tax paid, individual utility will rise. Conversely, when the government reduces or eliminates an income tax rate, the resulting reduction in tax revenue for funding useful government projects will create a negative income effect that offsets the positive income effect of the tax change. If the value of the lost government spending exceeds the reduction in taxes paid, utility will fall.

It is important to note that the example in which an increase in income tax yields beneficial forms of increased government spending posits spending of the kind that translates into an equivalent reduction in the cost of some item on which the individual already spends. The converse example would be a tax cut that requires the individual to spend his tax saving on something previously provided "free" by the government. Because plausible examples are hard to find, it seems likely that income taxes will exert income as well as substitution effects. Also, the substitution effect will more and more dominate the income effect as the tax rate approaches 100%.

The next question is how the imposition of an income tax will affect the demand for labor. Again, suppose that there is no income tax and Adam has a job that pays $50 per hour. We know from Chapter 5 that Adam will adjust his work effort so that

$$MRS_{LeLay} = w = \$50, \tag{7.3}$$

and his employer will adjust the quantity of labor purchased from Adam so that

$$MP_l = w = \$50. \tag{7.4}$$

Thus, as shown in Chapter 6, the socially optimal amount of labor is provided, inasmuch as

$$MRS_{LeLay} = MP_l = \$50. \tag{7.5}$$

the income generated by another hour of labor time is just equal to the income that Adam would have to receive in order to be willing to provide that hour of labor time.

Now suppose the government imposes a 50% tax on labor income. Adam's after-tax wage rate w_{at} now equals 50% of his before tax wage rate w_{bt}:

$$a_{at} = w_{bt}(1-t) = \$100(1-0.5) = \$50. \tag{7.6}$$

Because he adjusts his work effort to his after-tax wage, he will set

$$MRS_{LeLay} = w_{at} = \$50, \tag{7.7}$$

while his employer sets

$$MP_l = w_{bt} = \$100. \tag{7.8}$$

It follows that

$$MRS_{LeLay} < MP_l. \tag{7.9}$$

The wage that Adam would have to receive, after taxes, in order to provide another hour of labor time is less than the additional income that the firm would receive by using that hour of labor time. As a result, the firm hires less than the socially optimal quantity of labor. As previously observed, the tax on labor income imposes a bias in favor of leisure and against work (see Figure 7.4).

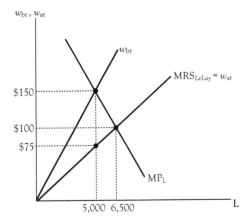

Figure 7.4 Effect of an income tax on the supply of labor

Without a tax, the quantity of work time hired by firms would be 6,500 hours at $100 per hour. Under a 50% income tax, the labor supply curve rotates in a counterclockwise direction so that the before-tax wage rate now diverges from the after-tax wage by $75 per hour. The quantity of labor hired falls to 5,000 hours, and the government collects $375,000 (= $75 × 5,000) in revenue.

Taxes on Capital Income

Capital income is a reward for saving. Our hypothetical taxpayer has a certain amount of disposable income, which she—we are bringing Eve back into the story—uses either for consumption or saving. She saves by using after-tax income to buy saving instruments like bank CDs, bank passbook saving accounts, government or corporate bonds, or corporate stocks. (She can also save by putting her money in a cookie jar, but that doesn't create any taxable capital income.) What she doesn't save, she uses for consumption or to pay taxes.

Earlier in this chapter, we expanded the framework of Chapter 3, where the individual had a certain amount of labor income that he had to divide between current and future consumption, to a revised framework in which the same individual had to take into account any taxes that were imposed on labor income.

Here we expand the framework of Chapter 4, where the choice between current and future consumption depends on r, p, and the individual's IES, to a revised framework that takes into account taxes that are imposed on capital income. We do so by introducing taxes on the income made possible by saving. Savers receive capital income by making financial capital provided through bank deposits and corporate stock and bond purchases available to firms. (For this purpose, we ignore institutions that provide financial capital.)

Businesses use financial capital provided through saving to engage in capital spending, that is, investment. In Chapter 5 we assumed that savers provided financial capital only through loans, which could be made via banks or directly to business investors. Here we expand the analysis to include financial capital provided via stock purchases.

In Chapter 5, the equilibrium r was determined through the interaction of a lender (Eve) and an investor (Adam). Recall that, in classical equilibrium, investment would expand until the marginal product of capital equals the real interest rate plus economic depreciation:

$$MP_k = r + d, \qquad (7.10)$$

where $r + d$ equals the cost of capital cc.

Now let's consider what happens when the government imposes a tax t on interest income. We return to the Garden of Eden, after the fall, where Eve saves and Adam invests. In Chapter 5, we considered the conditions that would have to be met in order for Adam and Eve to reach equilibrium in their saving–investment calculus. But now we have to think about how the imposition of this tax might affect the cost of capital cc and what we will call the after-tax return to saving r_{at}. Let the before-tax interest rate enjoyed by Eve, which is to say, the interest rate that Adam actually pays, be r_{bt}. Then

$$r_{at} = r_{bt}(1 - t). \qquad (7.11)$$

In order for Eve's after-tax return on her saving to match the return r she got before the tax was imposed, r_{bt} must be high enough so that $r_{at} = r$. Thus it must be true that

$$r_{bt} = \frac{r}{1-t}. \qquad (7.12)$$

What does this mean for the cost of capital? The answer is that it depends on whether Adam can deduct the cost of capital from his taxable income. Suppose that Eve passes on the full amount of the tax to Adam by charging the interest rate r_{bt} as defined in equation (7.12), and suppose that Adam can deduct both the interest he pays Eve and economic depreciation. (In fact, the amount of depreciation that can be deducted will differ from economic depreciation, but we ignore this distinction for now.) If Adam's business income is taxed at the same rate as Eve's interest earnings are taxed, then cc becomes

$$cc = \frac{r+d}{1-t}(1-t) = r+d. \qquad (7.13)$$

There is no effect on the cost of capital if Adam uses debt financing to acquire the funds needed to buy his oven and if depreciation and the cost of debt financing is fully deductible.

Now let's examine what Eve is doing about her saving decision. Eve adjusts her saving until

$$MRS_{c_t c_{t+1}} = (1 + r). \qquad (7.14)$$

For his part, Adam adjusts his capital holdings until

$$MP_k = cc. \qquad (7.15)$$

Because

$$cc = r + d \qquad (7.16)$$

$$MRS_{c_t c_{t+1}} = 1 + MP_k - d, \qquad (7.17)$$

which we previously saw as equation (5.31) in Chapter 5.

The value to the firm of another dollar of capital spending is just equal to the increment in future consumption that a saver would have to receive in order to make a dollar available to the firm for the purpose of buying new capital.

Taxing Corporate Income

The matter becomes more complicated when Adam obtains financing by offering ownership in the firm rather than by just borrowing the money. The traditional arrangement is to form a corporation and use equity capital (i.e., sell stock) to finance capital purchases.

Let's assume that the after-tax return to Eve for providing debt financing is 5% and that Adam already has four pizza ovens for his business but now wishes to secure equity financing to buy a fifth oven. He wants to make a stock offering that will bring in enough cash so he can buy an oven costing $1,000, which, we assume, depreciates at the rate of 10% per year. Adam plans to sell the stock to Eve and to compensate her for her stock purchase by paying out the entire return on the additional oven as a dividend.

If there were no taxes to be paid on this return and if Eve's stock purchase were for $1,000, Adam would pay her an annual dividend of $150, which would be just high enough to cover her expected after-tax return of 5% plus another 10% to cover the annual loss in share value owing to the depreciation of the oven.

However, there will be taxes to pay, which makes all the difference between this and the arrangement in which Adam relied on debt financing. In fact, there will be two taxes to pay as the profit generated by the purchase of the fifth oven makes its way to Eve's pockets. First there is the corporation income tax, imposed at a rate of t_c, which we will assume to be 21% (which is the top statutory rate on U.S. corporations). Then there is the individual income tax rate, t_{div}, that Eve will have to pay on the dividends she receives, which in her assumed tax bracket, would be 15%. (There would ordinarily be a state corporation income tax for Adam to pay and a state income tax for Eve to pay, but we will ignore those taxes here.)

So the question is what rate of return would Eve have to get on her stock in order to make it worth her while to buy that stock rather than put her money in the bank. This rate of return is now the cost of capital to Adam, in this instance the cost of raising financial capital by selling stock. As before, we will designate this cost of capital as cc. In order to determine cc, we need to figure out how much in taxes Adam and Eve will have to pay before Eve sees a dollar of reward for buying stock in Adam's company.

Let's start with the tax treatment of depreciation on the oven. If the IRS lets Adam depreciate the oven over a period of five years, he will be able to reduce his company's taxable income by 1/5 of $1,000, or by $200, for five years after he buys the oven, beginning with the first tax year for which he can take the depreciation. At a tax rate of 21% (per the Tax Cuts and Jobs Act of 2017), that's an annual saving of $42 (= 0.21 × $200). If the discount rate is 5%, the present value of this saving is

$$PV_d = \frac{\$42}{1.05^1} + \frac{\$42}{1.05^2} + \frac{\$42}{1.05^3} + \frac{\$42}{1.05^4} + \frac{\$42}{1.05^5} = \$181.84. \quad (7.18)$$

In effect, the depreciation allowance reduces the cost of buying the oven by 18.18%, from $1,000 to $818.16.

We will designate the fraction of the cost of buying a capital asset that the investor saves by depreciating that asset as f_d (here equal to 18.18%). We will ignore any tax saving that Adam might enjoy by taking advantage of an investment tax credit or some other such benefit that the tax laws might allow.

The fact that Adam can depreciate his capital for tax purposes makes it cheaper for him to raise financial capital. Let's imagine that the tax laws permitted Adam to depreciate a new oven in the manner just described. Because Adam would, we also assume, have to pay corporate taxes on income yielded by other investments, he could still reduce his overall tax liability by $42 for each of the next five years just as we previously noted. Adam could use the resulting stream of tax savings to reduce the amount of financial capital he needs to raise in order to buy the oven. Thus in this example, he needs to raise only $818.16.

Now let's see where we are in computing the tax burden on Adam's business and on Eve's pocketbook that results when she provides enough financing in order for him to buy the oven. First, if the oven generates a profit, his corporate tax liability for receiving the income generated by the purchase of the oven will be

$$tax_c = t_c \times inc, \quad (7.19)$$

where t_c is the corporation tax rate that applies to income generated by this purchase. Because Adam distributes all of his after-tax corporate income as dividends, Eve gets a before-tax dividend equal to

$$div_{bt} = inc - tax_c.$$ (7.20)

So

$$div_{bt} = inc(1 - t_c).$$ (7.21)

Eve will pay a tax on her dividend of

$$tax_d = t_d div_{bt}.$$ (7.22)

Her after-tax dividend will then be

$$div_{at} = div_{bt} - tax_d = [inc(1 - t_c)][1 - t_d].$$ (7.23)

We know that Eve has to end up with an after-tax dividend high enough to justify taking $818.16 out of the bank and using it to buy pizza stock. That after-tax dividend is

$$div_{at} = p_c(1 - f_d)(r + d).$$ (7.24)

In order for Eve to receive this after-tax dividend, Adam must receive income from the purchase of the oven of

$$inc = \left[\frac{p_c(1 - f_d)(r + d)}{1 - t_d} \right]\left[\frac{1}{1 - t_c} \right].$$ (7.25)

Using the information we have about this investment, the income Adam must receive is

$$inc = \left[\frac{\$1,000(1 - 0.1818)(0.05 + 0.1)}{1 + 0.15} \right]\left[\frac{1}{1 - 0.21} \right] = \$182.76.$$ (7.26)

The pizza oven must generate a profit of $182.76 in order to leave Eve with her required after-tax dividend. Adam's corporation pays 21% or $38.38 in taxes on its income, leaving it with $144.38 in after-tax income to be distributed to Eve as a dividend, on which she pays taxes of $21.66 (= 0.15*144.38), leaving her with $122.72, which is required after-tax income. Because $122.72/818.16 = 15%, this leaves her with just enough to earn a 15% return on her purchase of $818.16 worth of Adam's Pizzeria stock.

The cost of capital to Adam is

$$cc = \frac{inc}{p_c}\left[\frac{(1-f_d)(r+d)}{1-t_d}\right]\left[\frac{1}{1-t_c}\right] \tag{7.27}$$

or, in this instance,

$$cc = \frac{\$182.76}{\$1,000} = \left[\frac{(1-0.1818)(0.05+0.1)}{1-0.15}\right]\left[\frac{1}{1-0.21}\right] = 18.27\%. \tag{7.28}$$

The investment must yield a return of 18.27% to make it worthwhile for Eve to furnish her equity capital. We can compute the *marginal effective tax rate* on her stock purchase as

$$t = 1 - \frac{(1-f_d)(r+d)}{cc}, \text{ or} \tag{7.29}$$

$$t = 1 - \frac{(1-0.1818)(0.05+0.1)}{0.1827} = 32.82\%. \tag{7.30}$$

Note that total taxes are $60.04, which is 32.82% (before rounding) of the $182.76 in income that the project needs to generate.

We can illustrate this graphically if we translate the forgoing results into their consequences for capital spending. See Figure 7.5. We have found that the cost per dollar of financial capital needed for Adam to

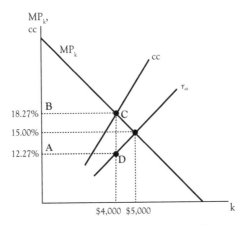

Figure 7.5 *Effect of a corporation income tax on the capital stock*

buy a pizza oven is 18.27¢, of which 32.82%, or 6¢, is paid in taxes. This means that savers receive only 12.27¢ after taxes, for every dollar of capital expenditure.

The cost of capital would be 15% but for the tax, in which case the firm would want to have five ovens, inasmuch as MP_k = 15% when k = $5,000. Instead the firm acquires only four ovens. The government receives 6¢ in taxes for every dollar of capital held by the firm, which in this example comes to $240, which is the size of area ABCD.

Table 7.1 provides some alternative computations of the cost of capital and the marginal effective tax rate (METR) for different assumptions about depreciation, the corporate tax rate, and the tax rate on dividends. One scenario sets the corporate tax rate at 35%, where it stood before the Tax Cuts and Jobs Act of 2017. A second lengthens the depreciation period to 15 years under current law. The last sets the dividend tax rate at 20%, which is the top rate under current law.

We see that the cost of capital rises with the dividend tax rate, the corporate tax rate, and the length of the depreciation period. The greater the cost of capital, the smaller the desired number of pizza ovens. This has implications for economic activity in that GDP is larger the larger the capital stock.

Now let's return to our current-law scenario, in which the corporate tax rate was 21%, the tax rate on dividends was 15% and the depreciation period was five years. As shown in Figure 7.5, the firm adjusts its capital stock until

$$MP_k = cc = 18.27\%. \tag{7.31}$$

Table 7.1 *Effects of alternative tax rates and depreciation periods*

Given			We can calculate cc and METR as follows:	
Dividend tax rate (%)	Corporate tax rate (%)	Depreciation period (years)	Cost of capital (%)	Marginal effective tax rate (%)
15	35	5	18.92	44.75
15	21	10	18.72	32.87
20	21	5	19.42	36.80

The saver offers financial capital only up to the point where

$$MRS_{c_t c_{t+1}} = 1 + r = 1.05. \tag{7.32}$$

Thus in this example,

$$MRS_{c_t c_{t+1}} = 1.05 < 1 + MR_k - d = 1.0892. \tag{7.33}$$

Equation (7.17) is not satisfied: The value to the firm of adding another dollar of capital is greater than the amount of future consumption with which savers would have to be compensated for providing that additional dollar. The taxes create a bias toward consumption and away from saving. In Figure 7.5, that bias is enough to discourage the firm from buying the fifth oven.

Untaxing Net Investment

Another approach to tax policy is to identify tax-rate changes that would keep tax revenues constant (i.e., be "revenue neutral") but nevertheless expand the economy. One way to do that would be to repeal the tax on income and replace it with a tax on consumption that is just high enough to keep revenues constant.

To see how this would work, let's begin with our stripped-down version of the NIPA income-expenditure equality from Chapter 2:

$$LAY + NW + D = C + I + G + NX. \tag{7.34}$$

The left-hand side is wages plus nonwage income plus depreciation of private capital, and the right-hand side is the sum of all expenditures that make up GDP. Let's assume, for this purpose, that nonwage income is asset income.

Under the income tax, the tax base is wage plus nonwage income, which is to say the left-hand side of equation (7.34).[2] Subtracting depreciation from both sides of the equation, we get

---

[2] In reality the existing income tax provides numerous deductions for nonwage income and is, therefore, a kind of compromise between a "pure" income tax and a consumption tax.

$$LAY + NW = C + \text{Net } I + G + NX. \tag{7.35}$$

National income and product accounting provides a reminder that taxes imposed on the income side of the equation, which is the left-hand side of equation (7.35), must fall equally on the expenditure side, which is the right-hand side.

Suppose, to begin with, that taxes are imposed on both wage and nonwage income and that Adam's pizza business has $1,000 in profits. In the preceding example, he would pay $210 in corporate income taxes. He would then have $790 left, which he could use to buy new capital or distribute to Eve in the form of dividends. If he chose to distribute the profits to Eve, she would, for her part, pay $118.50 (= 0.15 × ($790)) in taxes on her $790 in dividends. Adam's $1,000 in profits would leave Eve with $671.50 in after-tax income. The government would collect $328.50 (= 32.85% of the $1,000 in profits) in revenue.

Now suppose that the government decides to tax only labor income. The tax base would be LAY or what we called "labor income" in Chapter 2. If Adam receives $1,000 in profits, he could distribute that amount to Eve in dividends, on which she would pay no taxes. Adam's $1,000 in profits would leave Eve with $1,000 in after-tax income, which she could apply either to consumption or to saving in the form of providing more financial capital to Adam. If she chose to use the same $1,000 to buy stock from Adam, he would be able to apply that entire amount to the purchase of a new capital, as if he had not distributed the profits to Eve in the first place. The tax base would be

$$LAY = C + \text{Net } I + G + NX - NW. \tag{7.36}$$

Suppose, alternatively, that the government taxed both wage and nonwage income but permitted firms to deduct capital expenditures from their taxable income. This is known as "expensing" investment. The tax base would be

$$LAY + NW - \text{Net } I = C + G + NX. \tag{7.37}$$

Note that, if $NW = \text{Net } I$, which would be the case if Adam used Eve's $1,000 to buy new capital, the tax base is the same, whether defined according to equation (7.36) or equation (7.37). Either way, it untaxes net investment, and the tax has the sole effect of reducing after-tax wages.

We can also rewrite equation (7.37) as follows, so that the tax falls only on C and G and that net exports are also untaxed:

$$C + G = LAY + NW - \text{Net } I - NX.^3 \qquad (7.38)$$

Were net exports to equal zero, the policies would yield the same tax base.

The policy of permitting firms to expense net investment is the core feature of flat tax proposals, notably those put forward by Robert Hall and Alvin Rabushka and by Steve Forbes (Hall and Rabushka 2007; Forbes 2005). The left-hand side of equation (7.37) provides the flat tax base. The best-known proposal for a consumption tax is the "FairTax," which would tax consumption through a national retail sales tax. The left-hand side of equation (7.38) provides the FairTax base.

Despite the hot dispute that can arise between "flat taxers" and "fair taxers," the two ideas have in common the fact that they untax net investment, which is the crucial consideration for tax policy. The argument for this policy lies in the expectation that the expansive effect of untaxing net investment would more than offset the contractive effect of raising the tax on labor. Both approaches pose some issues for the monetary authorities, which issues we take up in Volume II, Chapter 1.

Evidence

David and Christina Romer argue persuasively that tax increases generally have negative economic effects:

> Our results indicate that tax changes have very large effects on output. Our baseline specification implies that an exogenous tax increase of one percent of GDP lowers real GDP by almost three percent. Our many robustness checks for the most part point to a slightly smaller decline, but one that is still typically over 2.5 percent. (Romer and Romer 2010, p. 799).

---

[3] Note that we assume that the tax would apply personal consumption expenditures and to all government purchases, not just the portion identified as government consumption expenditures in the NIPA.

In another study, Romer and Romer conclude from the evidence "that taxes are indeed distortionary: the null hypothesis of no effect is overwhelmingly rejected." On the other hand, they find that "the distortions are small." Their "baseline estimate of the elasticity of taxable income with respect to the after-tax share is approximately 0.2. This is considerably smaller than the findings of postwar studies (though generally within their confidence intervals). Finally, the estimates are extremely robust" (C. D. Romer and Romer 2013, p. 39).

In a study on *How the Supply of Labor Responds to Changes in Fiscal Policy*, the Congressional Budget Office contrasted the effects of short-term and permanent tax changes:

> Suppose first that the hypothetical 2 percentage-point increase in the tax rate applied to all income is imposed for just one year. People's desire to work less during that year, combined with their willingness to substitute work and consumption between that year and future years, causes them to reduce the labor supply by 1.11 percent during the year of the tax surcharge, on the basis of CBO's central estimate of the Frisch elasticity. The proportional change in the overall labor supply is about equal to the change in the supply of labor by an average person, which would be 1.16 percent (the product of a Frisch elasticity of 0.40 and a 2.9 percent decline in the after-tax marginal wage rate) (Congressional Budget Office 2012b, p. 7).[4]

---

[4] In any discussion of tax policy, it is important to distinguish marginal tax rates from average tax rates. Consider a married couple who set out to calculate their 2017 federal income tax bill, and suppose that they find that their 2017 taxable income was $150,000. Using the IRS tax tables we find that they owe the government $29,466. Their average tax rate equals their tax bill divided by their taxable income, or 19.64%. But their marginal tax rate is 28%, given that they find themselves in the 28% income tax bracket. The distinction is important for assessing how their tax schedule affects their willingness to work. Suppose that our couple (Adam and Eve, of course) had to decide on January 1, 2018, whether one of them should take a consulting job that would pay $3,600. Because taking that job would push them into the 28% tax bracket, they must compute the after-tax reward for taking that job on the assumption that doing so would add $1,008 (= 0.28 × $3,600) to their taxes. What matters is their marginal, not their average tax rate. From this example, we see why economists who attempt to

For a permanent tax change, the result is far less robust:

> If, instead, the surtax is permanent, people's desire to work less causes them to reduce the overall labor supply by 0.83 percent, according to CBO's life-cycle model. That change equals what would result from a 2.9 percent reduction in the after-tax marginal wage rate and a substitution elasticity of just under 0.29 (2.9*0.286=0.83) (Congressional Budget Office 2012b, p. 7).

Mathias Trabandt and Harald Uhlig estimated the Laffer curve for the United States and a group of 14 European Union countries. They found that

> for the US model 32% of a labor tax cut and 51% of a capital tax cut are self-financing in the steady state. In the EU-14 economy 54% of a labor tax cut and 79% of a capital tax cut are self-financing. We show that lowering the capital income tax as well as raising the labor income tax results in higher tax revenue in both the US and the EU-14, i.e. in terms of a "Laffer hill," both the US and the EU-14 are on the wrong side of the peak [the side where the curve is downward sloping] with respect to their capital tax rates (Trabandt and Uhlig 2009, p. 3).

On the basis of this finding, the United States could expand the economy *and* increase tax revenues by untaxing net investment.

Having considered the effects of taxes on the economy, we turn next to the government expenditures for which taxes are imposed.

---

determine the effects of tax-law changes on economic behavior focus on changes in marginal, not average rates. Using evidence on changing average rates to measure economic effects is misleading because average rates are calculated by dividing tax liabilities by taxable income, which itself depends on how changes in marginal rates affect economic behavior.

CHAPTER 8

Government Spending

Taxes affect the economic choices made by individuals, but so do the expenditures for which the taxes are collected. Government spends money by purchasing goods and services and by providing benefits in the form of transfer payments and subsidies. We use the letter G to denote government purchase of goods and services and T to denote taxes minus transfer payments.

In our simplified version of NIPA accounting, we consider all government purchases to be consumption spending, such as spending on the wages for government workers. But it is important to recognize, as do the NIPA accounts, that some government purchases are for infrastructure projects like roads and schools.

Here we will consider government spending on transfer payments, consumption, and infrastructure. Spending on consumption and infrastructure involves the diversion of factor services from the private sector to government purchases. Transfer payments simply take money provided by taxpayers and then redistribute that money to recipients in the form of social or safety-net benefits.

Transfer Payments

Let's start with transfer payments. We have seen how income taxes reduce the cost of leisure and thus impel workers to substitute leisure for work. Transfer payments can have the same effect. Means-tested transfer payments create a disincentive to increase earnings since eligibility for benefits depends on keeping earnings below a certain level.

In Chapter 2, we showed that total transfer payments by all U.S. government entities amounted to $2,786 billion in 2016. The Congressional Budget Office has put total means-tested federal transfer payments at $745 billion for fiscal year 2017 (CBO 2017a). This is made up in part of expenditures on Medicaid ($389 billion) and Supplemental Security Income (SSI) benefits for disabled persons at $55 billion (CBO 2017b). About 74 million people were enrolled in Medicaid and Children's Health Insurance Program (CHIP) in December 2017 (Medicaid 2017), which provided $550 billion in benefits to 67 million enrollees (MACStats: Medicaid and CHIP Data Book 2017). The U.S. Department of Agriculture reports that it provided $64 billion in SNAP benefits (previously known as "food stamps") in FY 2017, for an average annual benefit of about $1,500 (USDA 2017). In 2018, eligible couples are entitled to $1,125 in SSI benefits per month (SSA 2018).

Medicaid eligibility rules vary from one state to another. In 2017, Massachusetts adults with incomes below 138 percent of the federal poverty level were eligible for Medicaid (KFF 2017). For SNAP benefits the U.S. threshold is 130 percent of the poverty level (CBPP 2018). Under 2018 rules, an individual who earns more than $1,180 per month is ineligible for SSI benefits (SSA, 2018).

Figure 8.1 charts the rise in U.S. transfer payments over the last 70 years. U.S. transfer payments were 3.01% of GDP in October 1947 and increased to 10.62% in October 2017.

Let's return to our worker, Adam, in order to illustrate how transfer payments like these affect the work–leisure calculus. Figure 8.2 shows how Adam offers less labor when government-provided benefits replace part of his wage. We assume that Adam pays no taxes. In the absence of government benefits, he is on curve AB, along which his wage rate is $50 per hour and along which he chooses point X, where he works for 12 hours and earns $600 and thus reaches his highest attainable level of utility U_1.

Figure 8.1 U.S. government transfer payments as a percent of GDP

Source: U.S. Bureau of Economic Analysis and Federal Reserve Bank of St. Louis.

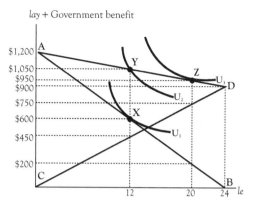

Figure 8.2 The replacement rate and labor supply

Now the government institutes a system of benefits under which he receives $900 if he doesn't work at all (i.e., sets his leisure at 24 hours) and gives up $0.75 in benefits for every dollar he earns. Under this system, he reduces his benefits to zero if he works all 24 hours.

Curve CD show how his benefits increase with leisure. Now Adam must find the optimal point on curve AD, which we obtain by adding curves AB and CD vertically and which shows the actual leisure–income choices before him. Adam could increase utility by keeping work and leisure constant and moving to point Y. But the fact that leisure is cheaper now causes him to move to point Z, where he now works only four hours. His total income rises to $950, of which $200 is labor income and the remaining $750 government benefits.

In his book *The Redistribution Recession,* Casey Mulligan shows that government policies subsidizing leisure have caused a reduction in the supply of labor (Mulligan 2012). In Mulligan's terminology, a recipient of safety-net benefits enjoys a *replacement rate*. The replacement rate is "the fraction of productivity that the average non-employed person receives in the form of means-tested benefits," and the self-reliance rate is "the fraction of lost productivity not replaced by means-tested benefits—and is merely 1 minus the replacement rate" (Mulligan 2012, p. 75). Thus in the forgoing example, the replacement rate *rr* is 75% (= $37.50/$50), and the self-reliance rate *srr* is 25% (= $12.50/$50) or 1 − *rr*.

Note that when the government benefits are introduced the individual's MRS_{LeLay} temporarily exceeds the amount he must sacrifice for another hour of leisure. Thus, he will expand his leisure and will continue to do so until he reaches point Z, where his MRS_{LeLay} has adjusted downward by enough so that

$$MRS_{LeLay} = w(1 - rr) = \$50(1 - 0.75) = 12.50, \qquad (8.1)$$

which equals the slope of curve AD.

Figure 8.1 illustrates the demand curve faced by an individual worker, for example, Adam. Adam's labor supply curve rotates upward from curve l_s^1 to curve l_s^2 as the social benefit is provided. At any quantity of labor, w now lies above Adam's MRS_{LeLay} by $\dfrac{rr}{1 - rr} MRS_{LeLay}$. In order to be willing to continue providing 12 units of labor, given that MRS_{LeLay} was \$50 before the benefit program, Adam would now have to receive a wage of $\$200\left(= \dfrac{1}{1 - 0.75}\$50\right)$. Then w would exceed the MRS_{LeLay} by $\$150\left(= \dfrac{0.75}{1 - 0.75}\$50\right)$.

We can think of the reduction in Adam's MRS_{LeLay} from w to $w(1 - rr)$ as having the same behavioral impact as the imposition of a tax on labor equal to rr, in which case we would write his after-tax wage rate as $w(1 - t) = w(1 - rr)$.

Figure 8.3 illustrates demand and supply for the labor market, where we determine the effect on hours worked of a benefit offered to a single worker. The quantity of labor provided by the worker falls from 12 to four hours. This is exactly parallel to what we could have expected if the government had imposed a 75% tax on the worker's labor.

In Figure 8.4, the market wage rate rises from \$50 to \$80 as a result of the institution of the benefit program. Now MRS_{LeLay} falls from \$80 to \$20 (= \$80 × (1 − 0.75)) and the quantity of labor provided by all workers falls from 1,200 to 400 hours, given that there are 100 workers with identical preferences. Again, the benefit program has the same effect as the imposition of a 75% tax on labor income.

Mulligan uses this framework to estimate how the expansion of safety-net programs over the period 2008 to 2009 reduced the self-reliance rate and, with it, the number of hours people are willing to work. Included in the safety-net programs he considers are SNAP, extensions

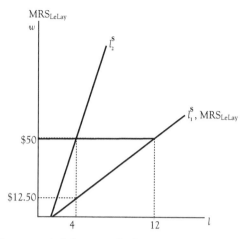

Figure 8.3 Decrease in labor supply I

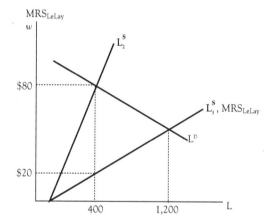

Figure 8.4 Decrease in labor supply L

of unemployment insurance benefits, and programs that offer debt for-giveness to home owners. Another team of economists found "that most of the persistent increase in unemployment in the great recession can be accounted for by the unprecedented extensions of unemployment benefit eligibility" (Hagedorn et al. 2013, p. 1).

Mulligan determines that the self-reliance rate was 59.6% before the recession began but then fell to 51.6% by the end of the recession in mid-2009. This was a change of

$$\ln(0.596) - \ln(0.516) = 14.4\%. \tag{8.2}$$

Mulligan finds that this decrease in the self-reliance rate caused hours worked in the fourth quarter of 2009 to be 10.5% less than they would have been without the safety-net expansion.

Using Mulligan's data, we can estimate the effect of the safety-net expansion on total hours worked. Table 8.1 reports (1) actual hours worked by private-sector workers in the fourth quarter of 2007 (according to the author's estimate), (2) an estimate of what hours worked would have been in the fourth quarter of 2009 had there been no expansion in the safety net, (3) actual hours worked in the fourth quarter of 2009, and (4) an estimate of what hours worked in the fourth quarter of 2009 would have been under Mulligan's assumptions about the sensitivity of hours worked to the calculated change in the self-reliance rate.

According to these data, workers put in 5.756 billion fewer hours of work in the fourth quarter of 2009, because of the safety-net expansion, than they would have put in, had there been no safety-net expansion. If we use the 2007 fourth quarter data on average weekly hours for private sector workers, this translates to an equivalent of 1.3 million workers who stayed out of the labor force in the fourth quarter of 2009 because of the safety-net expansion.[1]

Had the safety-net legislation not been adopted, the labor force participation rate (LFPR) would, according to these findings, have been 65.3% in

Table 8.1 Changes in hours worked under safety net expansion

Quarter	Total hours worked (billions)	Change from 2007. Q4 hours (billions)	Change from 2007.Q4 hours (%)
2007.Q4 actual hours	52.145	-	-
2009.Q4 estimated (no safety-net expansion) hours	54.492	2.347	4.5
2009.Q4 actual hours	47.817	−4.328	−8.3
2009.Q4 estimated (safety-net expansion)	48.756	−3.389	−6.5

---

[1] According to the U.S. Bureau of Labor Statistics, average weekly hours for private sector workers was 34.4 in the fourth quarter of 2007.

the fourth quarter of 2009, higher than the actual LFPR, which was 64.8%. The LFPR was 62.9% in June 2018.[2]

Mulligan puts the shrinkage in output from the fourth quarter of 2007 to fourth quarter of 2009 at 3.9% and the shrinkage in work hours at 8.3%. His model shows a predicted 2.7% shrinkage in output and a 6.5% shrinkage in employment (Mulligan 2012, p. 103). He attributes the difference to factors not explained by his model.

Government Consumption

The relevant question when it comes to government consumption is whether individuals see that consumption as providing a substitute for consumption in the private sector. As discussed in Chapter 7, a tax imposed to fund, say, government-provided health care provides benefits that reduce the need to spend on privately provided health care. If (and I don't recommend this) the government, for example, imposed a tax to raise revenue that would be used to provide free access to the clinics like the CVS Minute Clinic near my house, then I would no longer have to pay to go to the private CVS clinic. This would largely offset the negative income effect of the higher tax and reduce my incentive to sacrifice leisure and to work more. Government spending on defense would not have this effect since that spending would not represent a direct cost saving similar to the cost saving on buying the services of the clinic.

Infrastructure Spending

Infrastructure spending (or, more generally, government capital spending) differs from other forms of government spending insofar as it affects the productivity of private capital. Government provision of a Minute Clinic is best considered to be government consumption, because like private consumption, it directly creates utility for individual

---

[2] Figure 5.11 in Volume II, Chapter 5 shows that the LFPR began what appears to be a long-term decline in the early 2000s. The start of the decline coincided with the recession of 2001 and has picked up speed since 2011 with the onset baby boomer retirements. Importantly, Mulligan adjusted for the aging of the population in making his estimates for 2007–2009.

consumers. Infrastructure spending, on the other hand, is best seen as increasing total factor productivity. Highway improvements increase Z in the Cobb-Douglas production function by increasing the productivity of trucks, which are part of the private capital stock, and of the workers who drive the trucks. Such improvements are akin to technical advances, such as improvements in the gas mileage of trucks, for their effects on the economy.

The dividing line between government consumption and government capital spending is, to be sure, arbitrary. Individual consumers benefit from highway improvements, too, in that such improvements shorten the time needed to get to a vacation destination and to work. But it makes sense to see government payment of wages for a nurse working at a Minute Clinic as consumption but government highway spending as investment.

There is a large body of work on the subject of measuring the productivity improvements from infrastructure spending. A trade report summarizes this literature and offers a range of estimates based on 68 studies. In this report, the authors conclude that a 1% rise in the public sector capital stock will lead to a 0.03% rise in productivity (Holtz-Eakin and Mandel 2015, p. 13). According to the BEA, general government fixed assets were worth $10,565 billion in 2016. GDP in 2016 equaled $18,625 billion. An expenditure of $100 billion on infrastructure would, by these numbers, add $5.3 billion to GDP.

Chapter 2 of Volume II ties government spending into government tax policy for a broader consideration of how the two combine to determine government fiscal policy.

Bibliography

Aizenman, J., and G.K. Pasricha. June 1, 2011. "The Net Fiscal Expenditure Stimulus in the U.S., 2008–9: Less than What You Might Think, and Less than the Fiscal Stimuli of Most OECD Countries." *The Economists' Voice* 8, no. 2.

Ball, L., and N.G. Mankiw. 2002. "The NAIRU in Theory and Practice." *Journal of Economic Perspectives* 16, no. 4, pp. 115–36.

Barnett, W.A. 2012. *Getting It Wrong: How Faulty Monetary Statistics Undermine the Fed, the Financial System, and the Economy.* MIT Press.

Barro, R.J., and H.I. Grossman. 1974. "Suppressed Inflation and the Supply Multiplier." *The Review of Economic Studies* 41, no. 1, pp. 87–104.

Barro, R.J., and H.I. Grossman. 1976. *Money, Employment and Inflation.* Cambridge Books.

Blinder, A.S. December 27, 2017. "Almost Everything is Wrong With the New Tax Law." *Wall Street Journal.*

Blinder, A.S. January 30, 2018. "Why Now is the Wrong Time to Increase the Deficit." *Wall Street Journal.*

Blinder, A.S. July 8, 2013. "The Economy Needs More Spending Now, Opinion Editorial." *Wall Street Journal.*

Bordo, M. September 27, 2012. "Financial Recessions Don't Lead to Weak Recoveries." *Wall Street Journal.*

Bordo, M.D., and J.G. Haubrich. June 2012. "Deep Recessions, Fast Recoveries, and Financial Crises: Evidence from the American Record." Working Paper 12-14.

Braun, R.A., and T. Jakajima. January 2012. "Making the Case for a Low Intertemporal Elasticiy of Substitution. Working Paper Series." Working Paper 2012-1.

Brooks, A.C. 2008. *Gross National Happiness.* New York, NY: Basic Books.

Carroll, C., J. Slacalek, and M. Sommer. 2012. "Dissecting Saving Dynamics: Measuring Wealth, Precautionary, and Credit Effects." IMF Working Papers, (WP/12/219). Washington, DC.

CBO. 2017a. "Congressional Budget Office's Projections of Federal Receipts and Expenditures in the National Income and Product Accounts." Retrieved from https://cbo.gov/system/files/115th-congress-2017-2018/reports/53083-nipas.pdf

CBO. 2017b. "Federal Spending for Means-Tested Programs, 2007 to 2027." Retrieved from https://cbo.gov/sites/default/files/115th-congress-2017-2018/reports/52405-means-tested-programs.pdf

CBPP. 2018. "A Quick Guide to SNAP Eligibility and Benefits." Retrieved from https://cbpp.org/research/food-assistance/a-quick-guide-to-snap-eligibility-and-benefits

Charlesworth, H.K. 1956. *The Economics of Repressed Inflation*. London, UK: Routledge.

Congressional Budget Office. 2012a. *Estimated Impact of the American Recovery and Reinvestment Act on Employment and Economic Output from October 2011 Through December 2011*. Washington DC: Congressional Budget Office.

Congressional Budget Office. 2012b. *How the Supply of Labor Responds to Changes in Fiscal Policy*. Washington, DC.

Easterly, W. 2001. *The Elusive Quest for Economic Growth*. Cambridge, MA: MIT Press.

Federal Reserve Bank of Minneapolis. 2014. "The Recession and the Recovery in Perspective." Retrieved from https://minneapolisfed.org/publications_papers/studies/recession_perspective/

Forbes, S. 2005. *Flat Tax Revolution: Using a Postcard to Abolish the IRS*. Washington, DC: Regnery.

Friedman, M. 1968. "The Role of Monetary Policy." *American Economic Review* LVIII.

Gordon, R.J. 2016. *The Rise and Fall of American Growth*. Princeton, NJ: Princeton University Press.

Gordon, R.J. August 2012. "Is U.S. Economic Growth Over: Faltering Innovation Confronts the Six Headwinds." NBER Working Papers, (Working Paper 18315). Cambridge, Massachusetts.

Gruber, J. 2013. "A Tax-Based Estimate of the Elasticity of Intertemporal Subsitution." *Quarterly Journal of Finance* 3, no. 1, pp. 1–20.

Hagedorn, M., F. Karahan, I. Manovskii, and K. Mitman. October 2013. "Unemployment Benefits and Unemployment in the Great Recession: The Role of Macro Effects." NBER Working Paper Series, (19499). Cambridge, Massachusetts.

Hall, R.E. 1988. "Intertemporal Substitution Effects." *Journal of Political Economy* 96, no. 2, pp. 339–57.

Hall, R.E., and A. Rabushka. 2007. *The Flat Tax*. Stanford: Hoover Institution.

Hall, K. 2017. *Letter to Richard Neal*. Washington DC.

Hanke, S. 2012. "It's the Money Supply, Stupid." Retrieved from http://realclearmarkets.com/blog/It%27s The Money Supply%2C Stupid%2C July 2012%5B1%5D.pdf

Hansen, A. 1939. "Economic Progress and Declining Population Growth." *The American Economic Review* XXIX.

Harberger, A. 1980. "Vignettes on the World Capital Market." *American Economic Review* 70, no. 2, pp. 330–37.

Heijdra, B.J., and F.V.D. Ploeg. 2002. *Foundations of Modern Macroeconomics.* Oxford, UK: Oxford University Press.

Hetzel, R.L. 2012. *The Great Recession: Market Failure or Policy Failure?* Cambridge, UK: Cambridge University Press.

Holtz-Eakin, D., and M. Mandel. July 6, 2015. *Dynamic Scoring and Infrastructure Spending.*

Hoover, K.D. 2008a. "Does Macroeconomics Need Microfoundations?" In *The Philosophy of Economics: An Anthology*, ed. D.M. Hausman. 3rd ed. Cambridge, UK: Cambridge University Press.

Hoover, K.D. 2008b. "Econometrics as Observation: The Lucas Critique and the Nature of Econometric Inference." In *The Philosophy of Economics: An Anthology*, ed. D.M. Hausman. 3rd ed. Cambridge, UK: Cambridge University Press.

Karabarbounis, L., and B. Neiman. 2013. "The Global Decline of the Labor Share." *The Quarterly Journal of Economics* 129, no. 1, pp. 61–103.

Keynes, J.M. 1936. *The General Theory of Employment, Interest, and Money.* London, UK: Macmillan.

KFF. 2017. "Where Are States Today? Medicaid and CHIP Eligibility Levels for Children, Pregnant Women, and Adults." Retrieved from https://kff.org/medicaid/fact-sheet/where-are-states-today-medicaid-and-chip/

Lee, K.k., and A. Jayadev. 2005. "Capital Account Liberalization, Growth and the Labor Share of Income: Reviewing and Extending the Cross-country Evidence." *Capital Flight and Capital Controls in Developing Countries. Cheltenham: Edward Elgar*, pp. 15–57.

Lowenstein, R. January 20, 2008. *New York Times Magazine.*

Medicaid and CHIP Data Book. 2017. Retrieved from https://macpac.gov/wp-content/uploads/2015/12/MACStats-Medicaid-CHIP-Data-Book-December-2017.pdf

Mandel, M., and B. Swanson. 2017. "The Coming Productivity Boom: Transforming the Physical Economy with Information." Retrieved from http://techceocouncil.org/clientuploads/reports/TCC%20Productivity%20Boom%20FINAL.pdf

McKie, J.L. 1965. "Causes and Conditions." *American Philosophical Quarterly* 2, no. 4, pp. 245–64.

Medicaid. 2017. "December 2017 Medicaid and CHIP Enrollment Data Highlights." Retrieved from https://medicaid.gov/medicaid/program-information/medicaid-and-chip-enrollment-data/report-highlights/index.html

Metcalf, M. 2017. "Boomers Are Retiring Rapidly: Are Successors Prepared?" *Forbes.* Retrieved from https://forbes.com/sites/forbescoachescouncil/2017/06/28/boomers-are-retiring-rapidly-are-successors-prepared/-316132344472

Mulligan, C.B. 2012. *The Redistribution Recession: How Labor Market Distortions Contracted the Economy.* Oxford, UK: Oxford University Press.

NCFRR. 2010. *The Moment of Truth.* Washington, DC: National Commission on Fiscal Responsibility and Reform. Retrieved from http://fiscalcommission.gov/

Piketty, T. 2014. *Capital in Twenty-First Century.* Cambridge, MA: Harvard University Press.

Rampell, C., and S. Dewan. 2014. "Study Suggests Recovery in U.S. Is Relatively Vita." Retrieved from http://cnbc.com/id/101312687

Reichling, F., and C. Whalen. 2012. "Review of Estimates of the Frisch Elasticity of Labor Supply." (Working Paper 2012-13). Washington, DC: Congressional Budget Office.

Reinhart, C.M., and K.S. Rogoff. 2009. *This Time is Different.* Princeton, NJ: Princeton University Press.

Rodriguez, F., and A. Jayadev. 2010. "The Declining Labor Share of Income." *Journal of Globalization and Development* 3, no. 2, pp. 1–18.

Romer, C.D., and D.H. Romer. 2010. "The Macroeconomic Effects of Tax Changes: Estimates Based on a New Measure of Fiscal Shocks." *American Economic Review* 100, pp. 763–801.

Romer, D. 2012. *Advanced Macroeconomics,* 4th ed. New York, NY: McGraw-Hill.

Romer, C.D., and D.H. Romer. September 2013. "The Incentive Effects of Marginal Tax Rates: Evidence from the Interwar Era." *American Economic Journal: Economic Policy* 6, no. 3, pp. 242–81.

Shapiro, M.D., and J. Slemrod. 2003. "Consumer Response to Tax Rebates." *American Economic Review* 93, no. 1, pp. 381–96.

Shapiro, M.D., and J. Slemrod. 2009. "Did the 2008 Tax Rebates Stimulate Spending?" *American Economic Review* 99, no. 2, pp. 374–79.

Solow, R.M. 1956. "A Contribution to the Theory of Growth." *The Quarterly Journal of Economics* 70, no. 1, pp. 65–94.

SSA. 2018. "A Guide to Supplemental Security Income (SSI) for Groups and Organizations." Retrieved from https://ssa.gov/pubs/EN-05-11015.pdf

Stiglitz, J. E., A. Sen, and J.P. Fitoussi. 2010. *Mis-Measuring Our Lives: Why GDP Doesn't Add Up.* New York, NY: The New Press.

Summers, L.H. 2014. "U.S. Economic Prospects: Secular Stagnation, Hysteresis, and the Zero Lower Bound." *Business Economics* 49, no. 2, pp. 65–73.

Taylor, J.B. 1998. "An Historical Analysis of Monetary Policy Rules (6768)." Retrieved from http://nber.org/chapters/c7419.pdf

Taylor, J.B. 2009. "The Lack of an Empirical Rationale for a Revival of Discretionary Fiscal Policy." *American Economic Review Papers & Proceedings* 99, no. 2, pp. 550–50.

Taylor, J.B. 2013. *First Principles: Five Keys to Restoring America's Prosperity.* New York, NY: W.W. Norton & Company.

Taylor, J.B. Undated. *An Empirical Analysis of the Revival of Fiscal Activism in the 2000s.* Discussion Paper, (10-031). Stanford University.

Trabandt, M., and H. Uhlig. September 2009. "How Far Are We From the Slippery Slope? The Laffer Curve." Revisited. NBER Working paper Series, (Working Paper 15343). Cambridge, Massachusetts.

USDA. 2017. "Supplemental Nutrition Assistance Program FY 2015–2018." Retrieved from https://fns-prod.azureedge.net/sites/default/files/pd/34SNAP monthly.pdf

About the Author

David G. Tuerck is professor of economics at Suffolk University in Boston and president of the Beacon Hill Institute for Public Policy Research. He has held a variety of academic, consulting, and research positions. His fields of study are public finance and macroeconomics. He has published several books and articles, made dozens of television and radio appearances, published numerous opinion editorials and testified, on three occasions, before the U.S. Congress, as well before several state legislatures.

Index

CPSIA information can be obtained
at www.ICGtesting.com
Printed in the USA
BVHW042111170119
538040BV00009B/19/P